Business and Emerging Technologies

Business and Emerging Technologies

George Baffour

BEP

BUSINESS EXPERT PRESS

Leader in applied, concise business books

Business and Emerging Technologies

Cover design by Charlene Kronstedt

Interior design by Exeter Premedia Services Private Ltd., Chennai, India

First published in 2021 by
Business Expert Press, LLC
222 East 46th Street, New York, NY 10017
www.businessexpertpress.com

ISBN-13: 978-1-63742-135-2 (paperback)
ISBN-13: 978-1-63742-136-9 (e-book)

Business Expert Press Collaborative Intelligence Collection

Collection ISSN: 2691-1779 (print)
Collection ISSN: 2691-1795 (electronic)

First edition: 2021

10 9 8 7 6 5 4 3 2 1

To Mum, Lou-Dione, and Bukola

Description

The pace of innovation in modern times is staggering, and with the time demands of many careers, it is easy to lose touch with current trends. If business professionals do not actively stay up to date with new developments, they can quickly become outmoded in the workplace or unattractive in the job market.

Business and Emerging Technologies is an extensive but straight-to-the-point guide designed to get business students and professionals up to speed with an electrifying range of emergent technologies and concepts in the shortest possible time. Readers will benefit from fluid, well-researched reviews of technologies like artificial intelligence, blockchain, cryptocurrencies, quantum computing, augmented reality, 3D printing, and nanotechnology, and will acquire the factual contexts needed to make insightful decisions as these technologies slowly, but surely, pop up in their occupational nexuses.

Keywords

industrial revolution; blockchain; cryptocurrency; bitcoin; quantum computing; artificial intelligence (AI); machine learning; 5G; Internet of Things (IoT); augmented reality (AR); nanotechnology; 3D printing; mobility; drones; driverless vehicles; alternative energy; solar; research and development (R&D); telepresence; emerging technologies; innovation labs; hubs

Contents

Foreword

I was fortunate to meet George Baffour in November 2017 in Kumasi, Ghana, where I delivered the 10th R. P. Baffour Memorial Lectures, at which event George was present, representing the family of Dr. R. P. Baffour, his grandfather. The late Dr. Robert Patrick Baffour was a pioneering Ghanaian engineer who was noted for having been the first Chairman of the Ghana Atomic Energy Commission and first Vice-Chancellor of the Kwame Nkrumah University of Science and Technology (KNUST), my alma mater. For his public and social services in the Gold Coast (then a Crown colony of the British Empire), Her Majesty, Queen Elizabeth II conferred on him the appointment to an Officer of the Most Excellent Order of the British Empire (OBE) during her Coronation Honors in 1953. Later, for his distinguished services to the nation in the areas of public service, higher education, engineering, and administration, the Republic of Ghana conferred on him the highest honor of the Order of the Volta in 1979.

I was happy therefore to make the acquaintance of the man's grandson. George and I met again at the University of Ghana in September 2018 during the Pan-Nkrumaist Convention, where George and I were both guest speakers. Since then, we have kept tabs on each other over many meals and on several occasions. I was proud of the young man when he informed me that he was writing a technology-oriented nonfiction book to be published by Business Expert Press.

The rationale for this book is something I feel very strongly about. I believe that this guide to cutting-edge technologies will be of immense benefit to MBA candidates and business executives all over the world who want to catch up with technological trends quickly. I encourage readers to delve into its chapters and unravel the principles behind popular emerging technologies such as blockchain, cryptocurrencies, artificial intelligence, quantum computing, and nanotechnology. Today's business world leans heavily on technological products and services; hence it is futile for any business executive to avoid gaining basic knowledge about the concepts behind these technologies.

Having been a pioneering co-inventor and co-innovator of fiberoptic technologies, along with Bob Maurer, Don Keck, and Peter Schultz, and having 14 patents to my name, I am a living testament to the transformative power of technology in the modern world. I am a Fellow of the American Institute of Chemical Engineers, an Associate Fellow of the American Institute of Aeronautics and Astronautics, a Fellow of the Ghana Institute of Engineers, and a member of other prestigious professional associations. In 2014, I was inducted as a Fellow of the National Academy of Inventors in the United States. I have worked on defense and nondefense applications of fiberoptics, nanotechnology, and other technologies, and founded U.S. companies, including Georgia Aerospace Systems Manufacturing (Atlanta). I have been on the boards of noteworthy companies and universities like MIT and have authored and/or edited several books on technology and innovation.

In short, I know all too well the essential role technology is playing and will continue to play in driving societal progress and stimulating commerce. It is my honor to author this foreword and to encourage business professionals to patronize and master the contents of this exemplary piece of work.

9th May 2021
Dr. Thomas O. Mensah

Acknowledgments

My sincere thanks go to a friend and mentor, the world-renowned Dr. Thomas O. Mensah, for his enthusiasm to write the foreword for this book, and to my peer reviewers, Dr. Amanda Nimon-Peters (Hult International Business School), Daniel K. Twimaise, Aditya P.V. Yeluru, and Jashan Jot Singh, who so graciously took time off their academic or personal schedules to examine my work and offer advice to enrich the book.

I want to thank my publishers, Business Expert Press, especially Scott Isenberg, Charlene Kronstedt, Sheri Dean, Melissa Yeager, and their production, editorial, and marketing teams. I also acknowledge the invaluable input of my collection editors, Dr. Jim Spohrer and Dr. Haluk Demirkan. Special recognition must go to Nigel and Rachel Wyatt of MagentaWord who first approached me about getting published at Business Expert Press, and who guided me through the vetting and approval process.

I must sincerely thank all those who granted me permission to feature their images in this book. They are the companies, SkyDrive, JetPack Aviation, SatoshiLabs (Trezor), Ledger, and SpaceX; the person, Yves Rossy; the university, TU Delft; and The Henry Ford. Without their kind permissions, this book would lack color. Special thanks go to SkyDrive for allowing me to feature their very handsome SD-XX on the cover.

My heartfelt appreciation goes to Stephen Turkson Sr., his wife Frederica, and their family for their immeasurable moral support while I wrote this book. I must thank Dr. L'Ouverture Octave Ellis and Ndeye Marie Christine Ndiaye for their objective encouragement. I am also grateful for the diverse contributions of my father, my close friends, and several others, including Moses K. Baiden Jr., Ifeanyi Christopher Oputa, Isioma Grace Okonye, Gloria Naa Yarborley Abbey, and the Baffour, Richter-Addo, Ayibowu, and allied families.

Introduction

It can be rather startling the extent to which novel technologies can impact society, and more specifically, businesses. To a business entity, new tech typically solves a problem or endows the organization with some financial or operational benefit; and to the tech-savvy employee, a new technology or process improvement can represent an exciting liberation from the drudgery of antiquated systems. For the uninitiated, out-of-the-loop professional however, the incursion of any new form of technology can bring with it the terrifying prospect of a painful adjustment process. Such a person will be apprehensive and fearful—rightly so—that failure to adapt could culminate in underperformance and ultimately threaten their job security.

Similarly, students enrolling in some top MBA programs may be surprised to discover that their case studies, projects, and assignments focus less on classical theory and more on changes in the market landscape arising from new innovations and technological developments. Here too, an inability to grasp trending tech concepts can spell the difference between academic distinction and underperformance.

These scenarios justify the rationale for this book. A deficient business professional or student faced with tech inadequacies may want to dive into rigorous research to catch up with everything all at once. Yet, the myriad of on- and offline resources can sometimes be so diffuse, and the technologies so numerous, that it becomes quite daunting to gain sufficient knowledge within a reasonable timeframe. This book attempts to solve that problem.

Business and Emerging Technologies is written to be a one-stop-shop guide, offering a somewhat oxymoronic *comprehensive overview* of an extensive range of technological innovations that are imminent, in development, or already on the market but rapidly evolving. Readers will find answers to the following questions:

- What technologies are expected to impact the business world over the next few decades?
- What industries will each innovation impact, and which business functions in particular?
- Which companies are developing, manufacturing, or deploying these technologies?
- How do I empower myself to fare well when these technologies appear in my working life?

This book is heavy with references, notes, and links. It goes beyond standard citation guidelines in order to give readers useful leads to further their research. In tech circles, some fringe ideas never even make it into traditional, scholarly, or gray literature before they are implemented or deployed. Also, some younger innovators use an amazing variety of avant-garde digital channels such as niche blogs, mailing lists, and op-eds to publicize tech developments. So also, this book uses lots of edgy, non-academic references, even those that have no guarantee of remaining at the same web address for much longer. Regardless, much effort has gone into trying to get as close to primary, conventional sources as possible.

CHAPTER 1

Four Industrial Revolutions

Throughout the ages, a host of innovations have steadily driven mankind forward, with each successive development contributing a little boost to the pace of human advancement. Novel ideas and inventions have helped us to tell direction, buy and sell in standard measures of value, print books, travel faster and further, see farther, see smaller, communicate beyond earshot, subdue inhospitable terrain, overcome the darkness of night, and cure disease. They include the compass, money, the printing press, the domestication of horses and camels, the telescope, magnifying lenses, gunpowder, the electric light, and antibiotics.

Yet, when we consider the large swathes of time involved and contrast them with the relatively infinitesimal span of an average human life, it is reasonable to conclude that these incremental leaps in human progress were quite sluggish at first. It was not until the 18th century that Western societies experienced an unprecedented collision of scientific advances and ingenious inventions, culminating in a giant leap forward that was perceptible within a single human lifetime. This has come to be called the First Industrial Revolution.

The First Industrial Revolution

Driven chiefly by the advent of steam power, an abundance of cheap coal, and advancements in iron production, the First Industrial Revolution—roughly 1760 to 1840[1]—was a period of increased production stemming from the proliferation of mechanization across numerous industries. This period of industrial enlightenment began in 18th-century Britain before

---

[1] Britannica, T. Editors of Encyclopaedia. 2021. "Industrial Revolution." *Encyclopedia Britannica*, www.britannica.com/event/Industrial-Revolution (accessed February 21, 2021).

spreading to continental Europe, America, and other places by the end of the first half of the 19th century. Machine tools and water- or steam-powered mechanization infiltrated many factories and created monumental surges in output, particularly in the textile industry, where the spinning mule and power loom (Figure 1.1) caused a massive boom that triggered growth in associated industries.[2]

Figure 1.1 An illustration of power loom weaving

Credit: T. Allom (illustrator) in History of the Cotton Manufacture in Great Britain by Sir Edward Baines (1835)[1] {PD-US}

These explosions in production rates in turn impacted supply chains and logistics, necessitating a substantial upgrade of transportation networks. In Britain, the development of steamboats warranted the construction of a vast network of over two thousand miles of canals,[3] which extended water transport into interior regions—complementing river and coastal shipping—for the transport of raw materials to factories,

---

[1] Baines, E. 2015. *History of the Cotton Manufacture in Great Britain.* Cambridge University Press. (H. Fisher, R. Fisher, and P. Jackson, 1835), p. 210.

[2] "Industrial Revolution." *History*, www.history.com/topics/industrial-revolution/industrial-revolution (accessed September 09, 2019).

[3] Johnson, B. 2021. "The Canals of Britain." *Historic UK*, www.historic-uk.com/HistoryMagazine/DestinationsUK/The-Canals-of-Britain/ (accessed April 24, 2021).

and of finished goods to the marketplace.[4] Concurrently, British roads, which were predominantly remnants of a Roman-built network that had not seen much expansion in almost two millennia,[5] finally saw radical improvements, cutting travel times dramatically. For example, a journey from London to Manchester, which in 1754 could take up to four and a half days, reduced to about 20 hours by 1830.[6]

Later, toward the end of the industrial revolution, the opening of the steam-hauled Stockton and Darlington Railway—25 miles connecting collieries near Shildon to Darlington and Stockton-on-Tees[7]—in September 1825[8] and the opening of the world's first intercity railway, the Liverpool and Manchester Railway, in September 1830, heralded the mainstream arrival of the steam locomotive.[9] This would set the stage for the future expansion of rail networks throughout most of the British Empire, much of continental Europe, and the New World, America.

The First Industrial Revolution had major impacts on demographics. In Britain, the surge in new industries and the concomitant demand for workers caused a swing in the economy from agriculture to industry. This shift drew people to a growing number of industrial cum manufacturing cities like Manchester and service centers like London and Edinburgh.[10] It is assumed that prior to 1760, over 75 percent of the

---

[4] Bogart, D. 2013. "The Transportation Revolution in Industrializing Britain: A Survey." Working Papers, Department of Economics, University of California-Irvine, no. 121306.

[5] Wilde, R. 2019. "The Development of Roads in the Industrial Revolution." *ThoughtCo*, www.thoughtco.com/development-of-roads-the-industrial-revolution-1221647 (accessed February 26, 2019).

[6] Smith, W. 1949. *An Economic Geography of Great Britain*, 153–154. London: Methuen & Co. Ltd.

[7] Mackenzie, L. July 20, 2018. "10 Facts About the Industrial Revolution." *History Hit*, www.historyhit.com/facts-about-the-industrial-revolution/

[8] "Stockton and Darlington Railway." *Head of Steam*, www.head-of-steam.co.uk/about-us/stockton-and-darlington-railway/ (accessed April 24, 2021).

[9] Sussman, H.L. 2009. *Victorian Technology: Invention, Innovation, and the Rise of the Machine*. Santa Barbara, CA: ABC-CLIO.

[10] Clark, G. 2002. "Shelter from the Storm: Housing and the Industrial Revolution, 1550–1909." *Journal of Economic History* 62, no. 2, 489–511. https://doi:10.1017/S0022050702000578

British population was engaged in agriculture,[11] but in 1801, 27.5 percent lived in a city or town with over 2,500 inhabitants,[12] and by 1851, over 50 percent of the population was urbanized.[13] Rapid urbanization fueled a barrage of infrastructural projects to provide water, sewage systems, and other utilities to the burgeoning urban population. Between 1812 and 1820, starting in London, economic and social life was further impacted by the introduction of gas lighting utilities, which enabled stores and factories to stay open longer and nighttime entertainment businesses to flourish.

With the significant severalfold increases in production across most industries,[14] economies surged and Britain, in particular, experienced sustained growth in per capita income. A growing middle class with disposable income began to emerge and, egged on by falling prices of goods,[15] they and the upper-class elite sparked a consumer revolution. Mass consumption flourished and onto the scene burst an assortment of luxury goods, domestic equipment, porcelain tableware, fine china, glassware, crockery, clothing, watches, personal gadgets, and miscellaneous mass-produced consumer items.[16]

But while, generally, standards of living rose for upper-class elite and the middle class, for the majority lower down the social ladder, they fell

---

[11] Clark, G. 2002. "The Agricultural Revolution and the Industrial Revolution, 1500–1912." Working Paper Davis: University of California, p. 2. http://faculty.econ.ucdavis.edu/faculty/gclark/papers/prod2002.pdf

[12] Page 688 of Wrigley, E.A. 1985. "Urban Growth and Agricultural Change: England and the Continent in the Early Modern Period." *The Journal of Interdisciplinary History* 15, no. 4, 683–728, https://doi:10.2307/204276

[13] Table 1 on page 126 of Law, C.M. 1967. "The Growth of Urban Population in England and Wales, 1801–1911." *Transactions, Institute of British Geographers* 41, 125–143, www.jstor.org/stable/pdf/621331.pdf

[14] Clark, G. 2005. "The British Industrial Revolution, 1760–1860." Davis: University of California, http://faculty.econ.ucdavis.edu/faculty/gclark/ecn110b/readings/ecn110b-chapter2-2005.pdf

[15] "Industrial Revolution-Classes of People." *Industrial Revolution Research*, www.industrialrevolutionresearch.com/industrial_revolution_classes_of_people.php (accessed April 24, 2021).

[16] White, M. October 14, 2009. "The Rise of Consumerism." British Library, www.bl.uk/georgian-britain/articles/the-rise-of-consumerism

severely.[17] In the textile industry for instance, workers—mostly unmarried women and children—toiled through 12- to 14-hour days for insufficient pay.[18] Additionally, the mad rush to cities and urban centers, and the unavailability of enough ready accommodation for newcomers, caused the emergence of congested slums where unsanitary conditions resulted in high death rates and outbreaks of cholera and typhoid.[19,20]

The First Industrial Revolution ebbed to an end from the late 1830s to about 1840 as industries matured, marked by a devastating worldwide cholera pandemic that claimed the lives of tens to hundreds of thousands.[21] It would be another three odd decades before the world would again encounter another jolt in industrial progress, the Second Industrial Revolution.

The Second Industrial Revolution

The Second Industrial Revolution, sometimes called the Technological Revolution, spanned the 44 odd years between 1870 to the beginning of World War I in 1914.[22] It was characterized by the mass production of steel, the proliferation of machine tools, the harnessing of electricity, and the development of the internal combustion engine, all in tandem with advancements and standardization in manufacturing and the widespread adoption of electrical mass communication, vis-à-vis the telegraph and telephone.

The development of the Bessemer process (Figure 1.2) enabled the mass production of steel and this fueled a surge in other industries, for

---

[17] Woodward, D. May 1981. "Wage Rates and Living Standards in Pre-Industrial England." *Past & Present* 91, no. 1, 28–46. https://doi.org/10.1093/past/91.1.28

[18] Beckert, S. 2014. *Empire of Cotton: A Global History*. US: Vintage Books Division, Penguin Random House.

[19] Dyos, H.J. 1967. "The Slums of Victorian London." *Victorian Studies* 11, no. 1, 5–40. www.jstor.org/stable/3825891?seq=1

[20] Wohl, A.S. 1977. *The Eternal Slum: Housing and Social Policy in Victorian London*, xxiv, 386.Studies in Urban History, no. 5. Montreal: McGill-Queen's University Press.

[21] Hays, J.N. 2005. *Epidemics and Pandemics: Their Impacts on Human History*. Santa Barbara, CA: ABC-CLIO.

[22] Mokyr, J. 1999. "The Second Industrial Revolution, 1870–1914." In *Storia dell'economia Mondiale*, ed. V. Castronovo, 219–245. Rome: Laterza publishing.

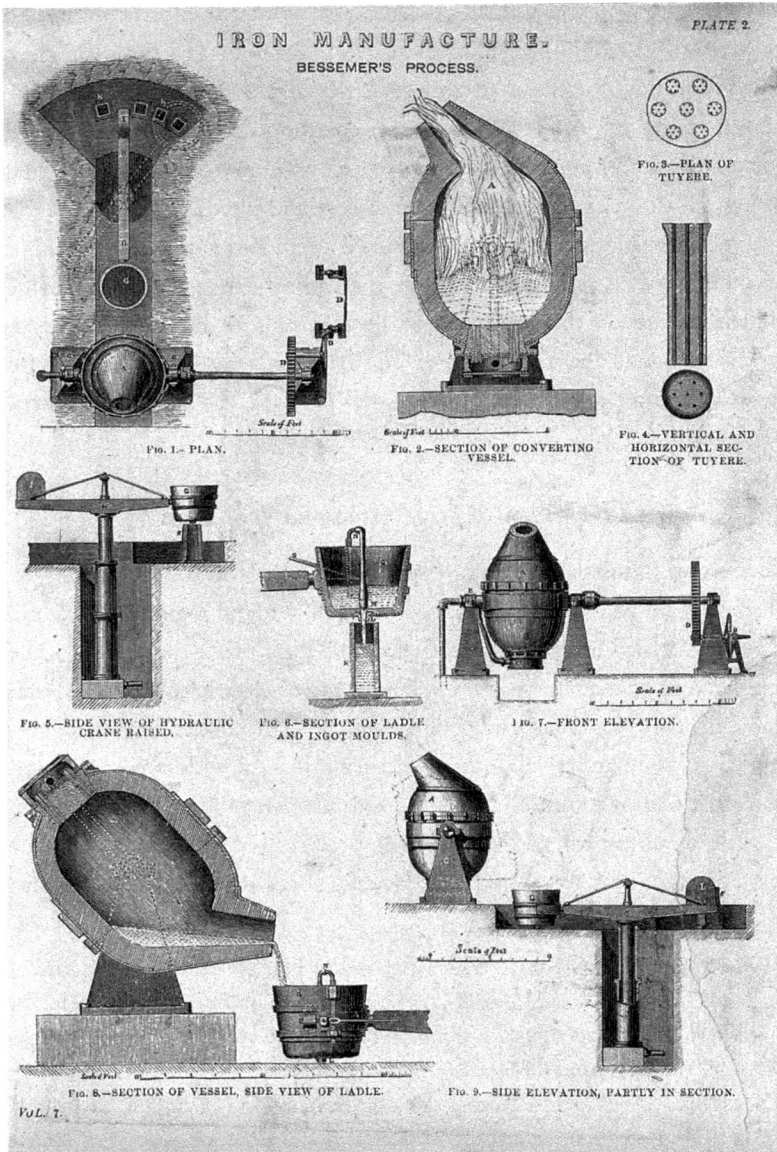

Figure 1.2 Iron: various machines involved in the Bessemer process of steel manufacture. Engraving c.1861

[23] https://wellcomecollection.org/works/ut2edzhm?wellcomeImagesUrl=/index-plus/image/V0024615ER.html

example, the expansion of railroad networks,[23] which in turn, being uneasily allied with telegraph lines,[24] grew the telegraph (and later, phone) network.[25] This mass transit of passengers, cargo, and electrical communication fostered a new wave of globalization. Railroads subdued the vast distances spanning some continents and brought new businesses to emerging markets and towns.[26] Following close behind, the telephone would soon build on the communication revolution of the telegraph, yet again bringing the world closer as commercial telephone exchanges began to open in 1878, first in New Haven (Connecticut), London, and Manchester.

Another incredible innovation dawned in the Second Industrial Revolution. Starting with its demonstration to the Newcastle Chemical Society in Newcastle upon Tyne (1878) then its first public deployment at the Savoy theater in Westminster City, London (1881), Sir Joseph Swan's incandescent light bulb began to bring light to Britain,[27] while in the United States, Thomas Edison's own version of the carbon filament bulb came into production in 1880, bringing electric lighting to North America.[28] The two visionaries joined forces and founded the Edison & Swan United Electric Light Company in 1883.[29]

---

[23] Ramirez, A. 2021. "Bessemer's Volcano and the Birth of Steel." *American Scientist*, www.americanscientist.org/article/bessemers-volcano-and-the-birth-of-steel (accessed April 24, 2021).

[24] Nonnenmacher, T. 2021. "History of the U.S. Telegraph Industry." *EH.net*, www.eh.net/encyclopedia/history-of-the-u-s-telegraph-industry/ (accessed April 24, 2021).

[25] Sidney, B., and M. Schwantes. 2019. *The Train and the Telegraph: A Revisionist History*, 224. Baltimore: Johns Hopkins University Press. https://doi.org/10.1177/0022526619879364

[26] Matusitz, J. 2009. "The Impact of the Railroad on American Society: A Communication Perspective of Technology." *PASOS: Journal of Tourism and Cultural Heritage* 7, no. 3, pp. 451–460.

[27] Swan, J.W. 2021. "Grace's Guide." www.gracesguide.co.uk/Joseph_Swan (accessed April 24, 2021).

[28] Palermo, E. August 17, 2017. "Who Invented the Light Bulb?" *Live Science*, www.livescience.com/43424-who-invented-the-light-bulb.html

[29] "Edison and Swan United Electric Light Co." *Grace's Guide*, www.gracesguide.co.uk/Edison_and_Swan_United_Electric_Light_Co (accessed April 24, 2021).

Meanwhile, after decades of development, electric technologies had become practical enough to support the maiden deployment of electric utilities. From buildings to streets to factories, electricity began to take hold, sparking the growth of large-scale power stations and the electric transmission and distribution infrastructure to support them.[30]

While the First Industrial Revolution had centered mainly on Britain and parts of continental Europe, the Second Industrial Revolution was of a much larger scale, extending into Germany, France, Italy, and reaching as far as Japan but centering chiefly on the United States. America played a leading role in the advancement of technology during the Second Industrial Revolution and its reputation as a country of innovation was further solidified by its hosting of several World's Fairs or Expositions during this period: Philadelphia's Centennial International Exhibition in 1876, Chicago's World's Columbian Exposition in 1893, Omaha's Trans-Mississippi and International Exposition in 1898, and the Louisiana Purchase Exposition in St. Louis in 1904.[31]

A hallmark of the Second Industrial Revolution was the dawn of the oil and gas industry. Prior to 1870, oil exploration and production had already commenced in several locations including Scotland, Baku in the Russian Empire, Persia, and Canada. In the United States, several oil companies had set up operations, notably Pennsylvania Rock Oil Company (1854), Seneca Oil Company (Connecticut, 1858), Virginia Petroleum Company (1859), and Vacuum Oil Company (1866). In 1870, at the start of the Second Industrial Revolution, John D. Rockefeller joined the fray and founded the Standard Oil Company in Cleveland, Ohio.[32] Petroleum production was focused principally on the refining of kerosene for illumination (lamps) and heating,[33] while the by-product

---

[30] "History of Electricity." *IER*, www.instituteforenergyresearch.org/history-electricity/ (accessed April 24, 2021).

[31] Findling, J. 2018. "World's Fair." *Encyclopedia Britannica*, www.britannica.com/topic/worlds-fair (accessed October 15, 2018).

[32] Vassiliou, M.S. 2009. *Historical Dictionary of the Petroleum Industry*, 13. Lanham, MD: Scarecrow Press [Rowman & Littlefield].

[33] McNeil, I. 1990. *An Encyclopedia of the History of Technology*. London: Routledge.

gasoline was considered unusable,[34] until two consecutive inventions came along that created a consistent demand for gasoline, which has persisted till now.

The development and refinement of the internal combustion engine by Étienne Lenoir (Paris) in 1859 and Nikolaus Otto (Germany) in 1878, respectively,[35] and the invention of the automobile by German engineer, Karl Benz, in 1886 changed the world forever. Benz's Patent Motorwagen (Figure 1.3) gained popularity after 1888,[36] but it was Henry Ford who would make the automobile widely available to the rest of the world.

Figure 1.3 Benz Patent-Motorwagen Model 1

Credit: DaimlerChrysler AG. License: Attribution-ShareAlike 3.0 Unported (CC BY-SA 3.0)

In December 1913, Ford's use of swappable parts, subdivided labor, and portable materials to develop a moving assembly line for the mass production of the Model T (Figure 1.4) shortened production time from

---

[34] Yergin, D. 1992. *The Prize: The Epic Quest for Oil, Money & Power*. NY: Simon & Schuster.

[35] Buchanan, R.A. 2020. "History of Technology." *Encyclopedia Britannica*, www.britannica.com/technology/history-of-technology (accessed November 18, 2020).

[36] "Company History." *Daimler*, www.daimler.com/company/tradition/company-history/1885-1886.html (accessed April 24, 2021).

over 12 hours to about 2.5 hours[37] and steadily brought the price down from 825 dollars (1908) to about 260 dollars in 1925, bringing the motor car within reach of the average American working-class family.

Ford's concept of combining 24-hour assembly lines, more shifts, and shorter hours per shift with high wages was revolutionary in its productivity and came to be known as Fordism.[38] Fordism and Ford's Five-Dollar Workday (Figure 1.5) quickly gained traction among competitors, auto part suppliers, and associated businesses who likewise raised their wages to keep up with Ford. This ultimately boosted living standards across America and lifted many working-class families into the middle class,[39] further boosting mass consumption.

Figure 1.4 The first Ford Model T (1908)

Credit: The New York Public Library[40]

---

[37] "Ford's Assembly Line Starts Rolling." *History*, www.history.com/this-day-in-history/fords-assembly-line-starts-rolling (accessed April 24, 2021).
[38] "The Moving Assembly Line and the Five-Dollar Workday." *Ford*, https://corporate.ford.com/articles/history/moving-assembly-line.html (accessed April 24, 2021).
[39] The Henry Ford. January 03, 2014. "Ford's Five-Dollar Day." *Blog*, www.thehenryford.org/explore/blog/fords-five-dollar-day
[40] The First Model T Ford. 1908. "Science, Industry and Business Library: General Collection, The New York Public Library." *New York Public Library Digital Collections*, https://digitalcollections.nypl.org/items/510d47e3-3be7-a3d9-e040-e00a18064a99 (accessed April 25, 2021).

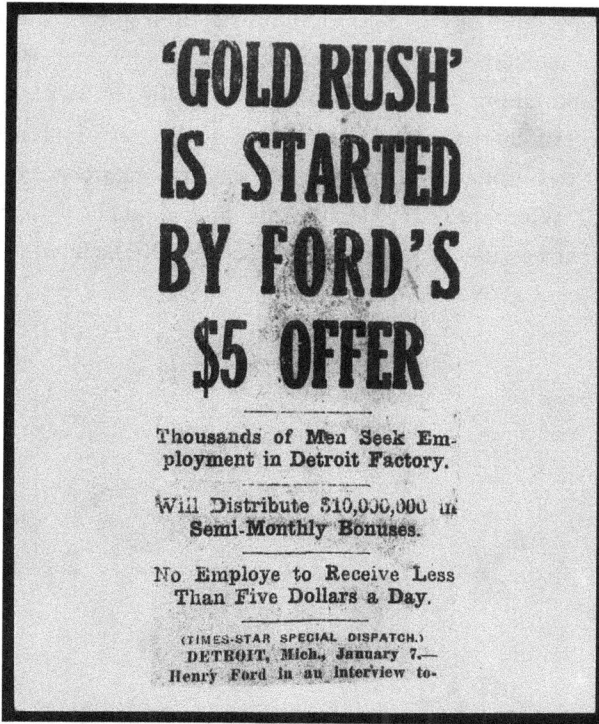

Figure 1.5 Ford's Five-Dollar Day features in Times-Star Special Dispatch (January 7, 1914)

Credit: From the Collections of The Henry Ford. Gift of Ford Motor Company[41]

Fossil fuels and internal combustion engines gained even more prominence from the development of compression-ignition engines by Herbert Akroyd Stuart (1886)[42] and Rudolf Diesel (1893), which ran on heavier oils than gasoline. Because of their efficiency and high power-to-weight ratios, diesel engines began to replace steam engines on ships and then locomotives, literally giving more oomph to the Second Industrial Revolution.[43]

---

[41] www.thehenryford.org/collections-and-research/digital-collections/artifact/99336

[42] "It's an Akroyd not a Diesel!" *The History Press*, www.chicagomanualofstyle.org/tools_citationguide/citation-guide-1.html (accessed April 24, 2021).

[43] Lienhard, J.H. 2000. *The Engines of Our Ingenuity: An Engineer Looks at Technology and Culture.* Oxford, UK: Oxford University Press.

Before the end of the Second Industrial Revolution, the internal combustion engine would facilitate the breaking of another grand frontier in transportation: flight. On December 17, 1903, Wilbur and Orville Wright successfully tested their Piper aircraft at Kill Devil Hills near Kitty Hawk, North Carolina (Figure 1.6), ushering in a vigorous age of powered flight.[44] Within just a few decades, mankind would be flying through the sound barrier (1947),[45] venturing into space (1961), and even landing on the moon in 1969 (Figure 1.7).

Figure 1.6 Orville Wright performs mankind's first powered, controlled flight, watched by his brother, Wilbur, at Kitty Hawk in North Carolina (December 17, 1903)

Credit: Library of Congress {PD-US}

Like the First Industrial Revolution, the Second Industrial Revolution too was followed by an economic dip and unpredictable global events—the ravages of World War I, the 1918 flu pandemic, the Great Depression, and more—until once again, a confluence of innovations culminated in a third giant leap for civilization, the Third Industrial Revolution.

---

[44] "1903-The First Flight." *Wright Brothers National Memorial*, National Park Service, www.nps.gov/wrbr/learn/historyculture/thefirstflight.htm (accessed April 24, 2021).

[45] Anderson, J.D. 1998. "Research in Supersonic Flight and the Breaking of the Sound Barrier." In *From Engineering Science to Big Science: The NACA and NASA Collier Trophy Research Project Winners*, ed. P.E. Mackm, 177–178. Washington, DC: NASA. https://history.nasa.gov/SP-4219/Chapter3.html

Figure 1.7 Astronaut Buzz Aldrin on the lunar surface during NASA's Apollo 11 mission (July 20, 1969)

Credit: NASA on The Commons @ Flickr Commons[46]

The Third Industrial Revolution

The Third Industrial Revolution or Digital Revolution, which experts generally place from 1950 to the present day, stemmed from key advances in electronics that enabled the development of high-speed computing and information and communications technology (ICT), culminating in the Internet. The Digital Revolution was marked by a global swing from analog electronics and mechanical technology to digital electronics and computing, all enabled by the development of semiconductor technology and related innovations. ICT, programmable logic controllers (PLCs), and robotics technology infiltrated many manufacturing industries, enabling unprecedented levels of automation in production.

Like the First and Second Industrial Revolutions, this Third Industrial Revolution also heralded the emergence of new sources of energy, namely nuclear and renewables such as solar and wind. The Digital Revolution was also marked by the breaking of new frontiers: human spaceflight and the landing of a man on another cosmic body, the moon.

---

[46] License: no known copyright restrictions. Details at www.flickr.com/commons/usage/

The advancement of space sciences also facilitated another revolution in mass communication: satellites. Telecommunications satellites enabled severalfold increases in the speed and coverage of telephone networks and television broadcasting. Also bursting onto the scene were weather and land-watching satellites, which made it easier to forecast weather or to track ocean levels and climate change.

One other breakthrough in telecommunications was fiberoptics: The transmission of electronic information via light pulses through tiny glass or plastic tubes called strands or fiber. In the 1960s, Charles Kuen Kao and George Alfred Hockham were the first scientists to promote the suitability of optical fibers for speedy, long-distance communication with low loss in signal strength.[47] American glass maker, Corning Glass Works, produced the first suitable optical fibers for communication. However, their fiber production was limited to two meters per second and even then, persistent problems with fiber quality caused massive production delays.

Ultimately, it was a Ghanaian American engineer, Thomas Mensah (author of the foreword to this book), joining the firm in 1983, who would craft and patent the principles and methods for manufacturing high-quality fiber at over 50 meters per second.[48] Like Henry Ford had done for the Model T decades earlier, Mensah's work revolutionized the production process, helping bring down the price of optical fiber to make it comparable to or cheaper than copper fiber, thus making this new technology available to the masses. Without fiberoptic cables beneath the oceans, we would not have the lightning-fast, global digital communications we enjoy today.

Advances in technology and communication directly and indirectly cause socioeconomic shifts as societies adjust to new lifestyles and information flows. The dawn of the Third Industrial Revolution coincided with marked changes in the social fabric of America and the world. In the United States, the civil rights movement rose to a climax in the 1960s,

---

[47] Hecht, J. 1999. *City of Light, The Story of Fiber Optics*, 114. NY: Oxford University Press.

[48] Brachmann, S. 2015. "Dr. Thomas Mensah: An Innovator of Fiber Optics Technologies." *IPWatchdog*, www.ipwatchdog.com/2015/02/01/dr-thomas-mensah-an-innovator-of-fiber-optics-technologies/id=54273/ (accessed February 01, 2015).

triggering the Civil Rights Act of 1964 and Voting Rights Act of 1965, but this period also saw the tragic assassinations of President John F. Kennedy in 1963, Dr. Martin Luther King Jr. in 1968, and Senator Robert F. Kennedy also in 1968.

In other parts of the globe, colonies under Britain, France, Spain, and Portugal fought for or gained independence from colonial rule. These included Ghana, Côte d'Ivoire, Nigeria, Sierra Leone, Algeria, Equatorial Guinea, Mozambique, and Jamaica. Meanwhile, the Vietnam War that had started in 1955 raged on till 1975 and other global conflicts followed in its stead. Truly, the Third Industrial Revolution and its technologies have overlapped with some of the most transformative social changes in the history of mankind.

The Rise of Modern Business

Having explored the three industrial revolutions in previous sections, it should now be obvious how critical a role technology has played in shaping society and the business world. Indeed, technological advancements helped mold the business profession as we know it today. During the First Industrial Revolution, the boom in mass production caused by steam power and industrial mechanization triggered the rapid evolution of new business processes and job functions in most sectors. Supply chain management, logistics, human resource management, and marketing began evolving toward what pertains today.

All too quickly, industry bosses had to adjust to recruiting larger workforces and minimizing employee turnover by balancing wage levels, workhours, and working conditions. Because of faster production speeds, procurement had to be fine-tuned into an art for batches of supplies and inputs to arrive at factories on specific schedules, without exceeding warehouse storage capacities. The distribution of finished goods also had to evolve to handle higher volumes per cycle. Quality assurance had to speed up to handle the inspection of greater quantities of finished products per cycle. All along these business functions, new job roles emerged, creating an explosion in new occupations and specialties.

Enterprises that effectively managed these and other variables made potentially huge gains, while entities that lagged could make monumental losses in no time at all, because of the larger quanta of inputs and outputs involved. The days of slow-paced, agrarian economies were over and a new age of industrial hubs had dawned. The growing prosperity of the period was complemented by the rising eminence of banks and financiers,[49] and the establishment of stock exchanges in London (1773),[50] Philadelphia (1790),[51] and New York (1792).[52]

The Second Industrial Revolution, which saw advances in rail, road, and ocean transport, as well as telegraph and telephone communication, conquered the vast distances of the globe and made it easier to do multinational business, thus dawning a new era of globalization. The ambiguity encountered in production and trade across diverse systems in different countries triggered the need for increased standardization, not only in machinery, machine tools, and technology but also in how businesses and their workforces were structured. With the surge in global business, there was a greater demand for skilled workers than what experience-based talent pools could provide. This necessitated the need for new fields of education focused exclusively on commerce and industry, and this fueled the popularization of business schools.

The world's first business school, *École Supérieure de Commercede Paris* (currently ESCP Business School)[53] had earlier been founded in Paris by Jean-Baptiste Say—who is largely credited with popularizing the term *entrepreneur*—in 1819 during the First Industrial Revolution.[54] But in 1881, during the Second Industrial Revolution, the Wharton School,

---

[49] "Industrial Revolution." *History*, www.history.com/topics/industrial-revolution/industrial-revolution (accessed September 9, 2019).

[50] "Our History." *London Stock Exchange*, www.londonstockexchange.com/discover/lseg/our-history (accessed April 24, 2021).

[51] "Stock Exchanges." *Library of Congress*, https://guides.loc.gov/wall-street-history/exchanges (accessed April 24, 2021).

[52] Waxman, O.B. 2017. "How a Financial Panic Helped Launch the New York Stock Exchange." *TIME*, https://time.com/4777959/buttonwood-agreement-stock-exchange/ (accessed May 17, 2017).

[53] https://escp.eu/paris

[54] Beattie, A. 2019. "Who Coined the Term 'Entrepreneur'?" *Investopedia*, www.investopedia.com/ask/answers/08/origin-of-entrepreneur.asp (accessed October 26, 2019).

attached to the University of Pennsylvania, became the United States' first business school and the world's first collegiate school of business.[55] Yet it was Harvard Business School, established in 1908, that offered the world's first Master of Business Administration (MBA) degree program and pioneered the Case Study Method for scrutinizing real-world business scenarios.[56] The rise of these and successive business schools contributed to the growing recognition of subjects such as management, finance, and economics as credible fields of academic endeavor, thereby fueling research, which in turn informed the progress of the business industry.

The field of business went on to experience further transformation during the Third Industrial Revolution. The Digital Revolution solidified the intimate interplay of business and technology. Documents and spreadsheets went digital. Letters and formal business correspondence leaped onto e-mails, faxes, SMS, MMS, and instant messaging apps. A host of business and enterprise resource planning (ERP) software emerged to aid functions in sales, supply chain, finance, accounting, and others. With the advent of Skype and other Voice over Internet Protocol (VoIP) services, formal business meetings and interviews could now be held remotely.

Presently, in the *new normal* brought on by Covid-19, remote working and telepresence are increasingly transforming how offices operate and how workforces collaborate. Besides that, modern business professionals, regardless of function, have to deal with technology at some point in their daily responsibilities; whether it be using a computer; recording and tracking customer visits on Salesforce; graphing data into Microsoft Excel and Tableau; or building presentations on Microsoft PowerPoint, Prezi, Keynote, or Google Slides. There are other business specialists and tech managers who routinely go beyond these to also manage innovation efforts by teams of engineers or developers. And then there are the business students who are having to learn about an ever-increasing range of technologies in order to ace their real-world academic projects.

---

[55] "History of Wharton." The Wharton School, The University of Pennsylvania, www.wharton.upenn.edu/history/ (accessed April 24, 2021).
[56] "History." About, Harvard Business School, www.hbs.edu/about/history/Pages/default.aspx (accessed April 24, 2021).

The point of all this is to illustrate that the field of modern international business is intimately tied to the technological advances that are burgeoning every quarter. Emerging technologies can influence, disrupt, or threaten industries and jobs. It is therefore in the interest of every keen business professional to be concerned with, interested in, or abreast with emerging technological innovations so as to foresee and prepare for impending changes to the business landscape before they happen.

In fact, there is vibrant chatter in academic and industry circles about yet another imminent or already-present industrial revolution that may transform the business world like never before.

A Fourth Industrial Revolution

The advent of the Digital Revolution triggered a radical change in the pace of societal advancement. While the rate of technological progress used to be steadily paced or relatively linear, the information and communications technologies of the Third Industrial Revolution fostered such rapid information processing and sharing that the global pace of innovation began to surge exponentially.

This growing rate of innovation and a host of other factors have led some experts to posit that we are on the brink—or in the early stages—of a fourth industrial revolution[57] that will herald new energy technologies, societal and workforce shifts, and a further melding of the digital and physical world. Industry 4.0 is expected to generate massive disruptions of—or democratizations in—production technologies, supply chains, mobility, health, and financial systems; and to force an unprecedented symbiosis between our real and virtual lifestyles. The enabling technologies of such a world are already with us or in development. A range of them are discussed in subsequent chapters.

---

[57] Schwab, K. 2016. "The Fourth Industrial Revolution: What It Means, How to Respond." *World Economic Forum*, www.weforum.org/agenda/2016/01/the-fourth-industrial-revolution-what-it-means-and-how-to-respond/ (accessed January 14, 2016).

CHAPTER 2

Blockchain

What Is Blockchain?

The concept behind blockchain technology was first described by Stuart Haber and W. Scott Stornetta in the article, *How to Time-Stamp a Digital Document* (1991)[1] in the Journal of Cryptology. In the article, they proposed procedures for using a "distributed network of users" and cryptographic hash functions to create a "digital safety-deposit box" or trusted timestamping service for digital data. Now, decades later, blockchain technology is a reality and is making groundbreaking impacts on the tech world, even though the technology is still evolving.

A blockchain is a digital ledger—a log of transactions or assets—consisting of discrete blocks of digital information that are linked in a chain and tagged in such a manner that blocks, once fixed to the chain, are infeasible to modify. Blocks hold timestamps, transactional data (such as currency, amounts, or quantities), and the digital signature of whoever is executing the transaction, usually without personal identifying information.

Each transaction is given a unique cryptographic code called a *hash*. Each block gets a hash, which is a math function derived from the information contained in that block, then the block also gets the hash of the block before it. This makes each block distinctly unique from any other. Once hashed, blocks are joined to a blockchain linearly in a chronological fashion, always being fixed to the end of the chain. Therefore, each block's position relative to preceding and succeeding blocks is permanent

---

[1] Haber, S., and W.S. Stornetta. 1991. "How to Time-Stamp a Digital Document." *Journal of Cryptology* 3, 99–111. https://doi.org/10.1007/BF00196791

and cannot be altered.[2] Depending on their size, some blocks can store hundreds or thousands of transactions.

Decentralized or Centralized

A blockchain is usually managed by a peer-to-peer (P2P) network of computers—each one called a node—which are responsible for verifying transactions and logging their information into blocks.[3] Thus, blockchains are often ascribed the quality of being *distributed* or *shared*. Blockchains can also be decentralized—which is often the case—or centralized. With decentralized blockchains, all participants on a ledger can perform or validate transactions, and this is typical of open or public ledgers where users are anonymous and represented by codes that are sometimes called public keys. In this case, protections in the form of qualifying proofs or tasks are usually designed into the system to ward off malicious actors from compromising the network.

Centralized blockchains, on the other hand, have smaller networks of only credible nodes whose identities are fully known and are therefore traceable if fraud is committed. Centralized blockchains are typically used by private entities and organizations or in regulated sectors such as banking, finance, or government,[4] but even in some of these industries, decentralized blockchains are gaining credibility.[5]

[2] Conway, L. 2020. "Blockchain Explained." *Investopedia*, www.investopedia.com/terms/b/blockchain.asp (accessed November 17, 2020).
[3] Sharma, T.K. 2021. "Blockchain & Role of P2P Network." *Blockchain Council*, www.blockchain-council.org/blockchain/blockchain-role-of-p2p-network/ (accessed April 25, 2021).
[4] Rutland, E. 2018. *Blockchain Byte*. R3 Research.
[5] Horlacher, C. 2017. "BankThink 'Centralized' Blockchain Projects are Doomed to Failure." *American Banker*, www.americanbanker.com/opinion/centralized-blockchain-projects-are-doomed-to-failure (accessed January 31, 2017).

Consensus

Distributed ledger technology (DLT) runs on the consensus of all (or most) of the nodes on a network,[6] which, if the network is decentralized, can number into thousands or millions. Each node obtains a copy of the entire blockchain on their computer and this is updated automatically for all users whenever the blockchain is amended by any one of them. The nodes work to independently confirm the veracity of transactional data before they are aggregated and added to a block.[7] The propagation of validation duties across a network rather than handling it centrally makes blockchain transparent and difficult to sabotage.

One cannot change the information in a block without altering its hash and getting caught, unless they change all succeeding hashes to cover their tracks, and even if this worked, a prospective hacker would need to replicate this on all (or most) copies of the blockchain on the thousands or millions of computers on the network. This is an impractical task for large, decentralized networks and would require an enormous or improbable amount of processing power.[8] Such an assault on a blockchain by a malevolent actor controlling over 50 percent of the computing power or validation functions of a network is termed a *51 percent attack*[9] and is rare but possible.[10]

---

[6] Wahab, A. 2018. "Consensus Protocols of Distributed Ledger Technology." www.medium.com/@wahabjawed/consensus-protocol-of-distributed-ledger-technology-c61526490e60 (accessed October 20, 2018).

[7] Stevens, A. 2018. "Distributed Ledger Consensus Explained." *Hackernoon*, https://hackernoon.com/distributed-ledger-consensus-explained-b0968d1ba087 (accessed April 30, 2018).

[8] Conway, L. 2019. "Blockchain Explained."

[9] Frankenfield, J. 2019. "51% Attack." *Investopedia*, www.investopedia.com/terms/1/51-attack.asp (accessed May 6, 2019).

[10] Lawler, J. 2020. "Punishing the Byzantine Fault: Application of US Law to a 51% Attack (or Threat)." https://medium.com/swlh/punishing-the-byzantine-fault-application-of-us-law-to-a-51-attack-or-threat-921bb0469247 (accessed January 7, 2020).

To further secure decentralized blockchains, new computers that want to enlist as nodes on the network have to pass consensus mechanisms, which are tests that require users to *prove* themselves, before they are approved to become nodes. Such consensus models are usually called proof of work or proof of stake.[11]

Uses and Threats

Blockchain, being a dependable way of recording all kinds of data and transactions, is apt for use in banking for money transfers, particularly because it is fast and convenient for securing international transactions across different time zones.[12] Blockchains can be used for smart contracts. A smart contract is a digital protocol programmed to negotiate, validate, or execute a contract once a set of requirements are fulfilled.[13] This is suitable for escrow services.[14] Another popular application of blockchain is cryptocurrency,[15] where decentralization eliminates excessive transaction fees otherwise tied to traditional, central fiscal authorities. Blockchain is

---

[11] Wolmarans, T. 2020. "Proof of Work vs. Proof of Stake: How Different Are They Really?" *Hackernoon,* https://hackernoon.com/proof-of-work-vs-proof-of-stake-how-different-are-they-really-yj3a3wtp (accessed October 4, 2020).

[12] "10 Use Cases of Blockchain Technology in Banking 2020." *Fintech News,* www.fintechnews.org/10-use-cases-of-blockchain-technology-in-banking-2020/ (accessed April 30, 2020).

[13] Rosic, A. 2021. "Smart Contracts: The Blockchain Technology That Will Replace Lawyers." *Blockgeeks,* https://blockgeeks.com/guides/smart-contracts/ (accessed April 27, 2021).

[14] Sharma, T.K. 2021. "How Blockchain Can Be Used in Escrow & How It Works?" *Blockchain Council,* www.blockchain-council.org/bitcoin/blockchain-can-used-escrow-works/ (accessed April 27, 2021).

[15] Marr, B. 2017. "A Short History of Bitcoin and Crypto Currency Everyone Should Read." *Forbes,* www.forbes.com/sites/bernardmarr/2017/12/06/a-short-history-of-bitcoin-and-crypto-currency-everyone-should-read/?sh=4a33a3803f27 (accessed December 6, 2017).

finding relevance in health care, for instance, in managing medical data access[16] and fostering transparency in clinical trials.[17] Likewise, it is finding application in supply chain management[18] and is even being explored for voting[19] and government transparency.[20]

Blockchain's security, accuracy, and efficiency are unparalleled but there can be some drawbacks.[21] The deployment of blockchain solutions can be costly[22] in the short run but, as with all new technologies, significant benefits can be reaped in the long run. The anonymity,

---

[16] Azaria, A., A. Ekblaw, T. Vieira, and A. Lippman. 2016. "MedRec: Using Blockchain for Medical Data Access and Permission Management." *2016 2nd International Conference on Open and Big Data (OBD),* Vienna: IEEE, pp. 25–30, doi:10.1109/OBD.2016.11

[17] Nugent, T., D. Upton, and M. Cimpoesu. 2016. "Improving Data Transparency in Clinical Trials Using Blockchain Smart Contracts [version 1; peer review: 3 approved]." *F1000Research* 5, 2541. https://doi.org/10.12688/f1000research.9756.1

[18] "Redesigning Trust: Blockchain, COVID-19 & Supply Chains of the Future." World Economic Forum, www.weforum.org/projects/redesigning-trust-blockchain-supply-chains-of-the-future (accessed April 27, 2021).

[19] Tatar, J. 2021. "How Blockchain Technology Can Change How We Vote." *The Balance,* https://www.thebalance.com/how-the-blockchain-will-change-how-we-vote-4012008 (accessed March 31, 2021).

[20] World Economic Forum. June 2020. *Exploring Blockchain Technology for Government Transparency: Blockchain-Based Public Procurement to Reduce Corruption.* Switzerland: World Economic Forum, www3.weforum.org/docs/WEF_Blockchain_Government_Transparency_Report_Supplementary%20Research.pdf (accessed June 2020).

[21] Golosova, J., and A. Romanovs. 2018. "The Advantages and Disadvantages of the Blockchain Technology." *2018 IEEE 6th Workshop on Advances in Information, Electronic and Electrical Engineering (AIEEE),* Vilnius: IEEE, 1–6, doi:10.1109/AIEEE.2018.8592253

[22] Iredale, G. 2020. "Top Disadvantages of Blockchain Technology." *101 Blockchains,* https://101blockchains.com/disadvantages-of-blockchain/ (accessed April 17, 2020).

semianonymity, or pseudonymity inherent in decentralized blockchains can be capitalized on by dubious parties for illicit transactions and the movement of dirty money.[23] This causes concern for many regulatory agencies and governments around the world who are still figuring out if and how to regulate blockchain and crypto assets.[24]

---

[23] Scheck, J., and S. Shifflett. 2018. "How Dirty Money Disappears into the Black Hole of Cryptocurrency." *The Wall Street Journal*, www.wsj.com/articles/how-dirty-money-disappears-into-the-black-hole-of-cryptocurrency-1538149743 (accessed September 28, 2018).

[24] Weinstein, J., A. Cohn, and C. Parker. 2019. "Promoting Innovation through Education: The Blockchain Industry, Law Enforcement and Regulators Work Towards a Common Goal." In *Global Legal Insights - Blockchain & Cryptocurrency Regulation, First Edition*, ed. J.N Dewey, 1–4. London: Rory Smith, Global Legal Group Ltd.

CHAPTER 3

Cryptocurrency

Cryptocurrencies, Coins, and Tokens

A cryptocurrency—a hybrid of the words, *cryptography* and *currency*—is a digital or virtual currency, unit of account, or medium of exchange, managed and secured by cryptography. Most cryptocurrencies are built on blockchain networks and are decentralized, providing immutability and transparency, without requiring a central authority or trusted third party.[1]

There are two main types of cryptocurrencies: Bitcoin and altcoins. Altcoins—alternative coins—are simply all other non-Bitcoin cryptocurrencies. And then there are tokens. Tokens are special altcoins created for use by specific enterprises and their investors or users. They are often issued as *security tokens* during the start-up phase of a blockchain-integrated business and can appreciate in value if the venture prospers. Tokens can also come in the form of *utility tokens*, which are typically exchangeable for a service or benefit from the issuing business.[2]

There are over 9,268 publicly traded cryptocurrencies with a total market value of just over $2 trillion of which Bitcoin is the largest single cryptocurrency, dominating 51.4 percent of the cryptocurrency market with a market cap of $1.05 billion.[3]

---

[1] Frankenfield, J. 2021. "Cryptocurrency." *Investopedia*, www.investopedia.com/terms/c/cryptocurrency.asp (accessed March 7, 2021).

[2] Frankenfield, J. 2021. "Altcoin." *Investopedia*, www.investopedia.com/terms/a/altcoin.asp (accessed April 11, 2021).

[3] Market capitalization information taken from https://coinmarketcap.com (accessed April 18, 2021).

Bitcoin (BTC/XBT)

Bitcoin is the trailblazing flagship of cryptocurrencies and is the world's first open-source digital payment system operating on decentralized, peer-to-peer blockchain technology. Bitcoin is fully public and is therefore issued and managed by its network of nodes, called miners, who verify transactions in exchange for bitcoins. This exempts Bitcoin from central control by banks and other authorities.[4]

Bitcoin was first proposed in the whitepaper, *Bitcoin: A Peer-to-Peer Electronic Cash System*,[5] by Satoshi Nakamoto, a supposed pseudonym for a person (or people) who as yet remains unidentified. The whitepaper was posted to a cryptography mailing list at metzdowd.com on October 31, 2008,[6] two months after the domain name bitcoin.org had been registered in August. In the whitepaper, Nakamoto detailed a blueprint of how to use blockchain to solve the double-spending dilemma inherent in electronic currency circles. The whitepaper outdoored the concept of a new asset the likes of which the world had never seen before: the decentralized digital currency, Bitcoin. Satoshi released version 0.1 of Bitcoin on January 3, 2009 with 30,000 lines of source code[7] and mined the *genesis block*—with a reward of the world's first 50 bitcoins—thereby launching the cryptocurrency. Satoshi actively worked on its development for over a year while it gained traction and more early adopters or miners, and then the mysterious founder slowly faded out from the project,[8] without

---

[4] Bitcoin.org, https://bitcoin.org/en/ (accessed April 25, 2021).

[5] Nakamoto, S. 2009. "Bitcoin: A Peer-to-Peer Electronic Cash System." https://bitcoin.org/bitcoin.pdf

[6] Nakamoto, S. 2008. "Bitcoin P2P e-cash Paper." www.metzdowd.com/pipermail/cryptography/2008-October/014810.html (accessed October 31, 2008).

[7] Bernard, Z., and K. Grace. 2021. "The Many Alleged Identities of Bitcoin's Mysterious Creator, Satoshi Nakamoto." *Business Insider*, www.businessinsider.com/bitcoin-history-cryptocurrency-satoshi-nakamoto-2017-12?IR=T, (accessed February 26, 2021).

[8] Wallace, B. 2011. "The Rise and Fall of Bitcoin." *WIRED*, www.wired.com/2011/11/mf-bitcoin/ (accessed November 23, 2011).

cashing out the one million bitcoins, which today[9] would make him (or her) the 21st richest person alive.[10]

The mystery of Satoshi Nakamoto's identity still persists today. Satoshi, who alleged on his P2P Foundation[11] profile to have been born on April 5, 1975, also claimed to be Japanese and living in Japan. Satoshi is a boy's name in Japan, so he is usually assumed to be a man. However, analysis of his vocabulary and spelling seems to reveal native proficiency in commonwealth English. Also, his sleeping (and working) hours, derived from the timings of his communications and the digital trail of his software development activities, seem to place him in the Greenwich Mean Time (GMT) zone of the United Kingdom and not the Japan Standard Time (JST) zone of Japan.[12]

Further investigations have led to the proposal of a host of candidates for his identity. Prominent among these is Dorian Nakamoto (born Satoshi Nakamoto),[13] a retired physicist trained at California State Polytechnic University in Pomona, and who worked as a systems engineer on classified defense projects and as a computer engineer for tech and financial information firms. Although he denies the claim, and so does a post from Satoshi's e-mail,[14] suspicion is further buttressed by the fact that Dorian's family home in Temple City in Los Angeles County was for nine years just a few blocks away from the home of Hal Finney, a developer and cryptographic innovator who was the first person to ever receive a bitcoin transaction from Satoshi and was the first person to improve the

---

[9] April 18, 2021.

[10] According to www.forbes.com/billionaires/ if having a net worth of about $56.38 billion.

[11] "Satoshi Nakamoto's Page." *P2P Foundation*, http://p2pfoundation.ning.com/profile/SatoshiNakamoto (accessed April 24, 2021).

[12] Mizrahi, A. 2020. "Who Is Satoshi Nakamoto? An Introduction to Bitcoin's Mysterious Founder." *Bitcoin.com*, https://news.bitcoin.com/satoshi-nakamoto-founder-of-bitcoin/ (accessed March 8, 2020).

[13] Mcgrath Goodman, L. 2014. "The Face Behind Bitcoin." *Newsweek*, www.newsweek.com/2014/03/14/face-behind-bitcoin-247957.html (accessed March 6, 2014).

[14] Mizrahi, A. n.d. "Who Is Satoshi Nakamoto? An Introduction to Bitcoin's Mysterious Founder."

Bitcoin source code after Satoshi. Hal Finney, himself another suspect in the Satoshi mystery, was an engineering graduate of Caltech and a cypherpunk[15] advocate but denied being Satoshi,[16] eventually dying of complications from amyotrophic lateral sclerosis (ALS) in 2014.

Other alleged suspects include Nick (Nicholas) Szabo who in 2005 had proposed the idea for *bit gold*[17]—a decentralized currency using principles similar to those eventually perfected by Bitcoin[18]—and who was in contact with Hal Finney. A graduate of George Washington University and University of Washington with a Juris Doctor degree in law and a bachelor's degree in computer science respectively, Nick has substantial experience in Internet security, e-commerce, software engineering,[19] and cryptography. He is also an originator of the phrase and concept of *smart contracts*, a core principle and feature underlying blockchain.[20] Despite this and other proofs, like his initials N. and S. being the same as Satoshi's, he has denied being Satoshi.

Another important suspect is Craig Wright, an Australian academic (remember our earlier commonwealth English reference) and businessman who actively claims to be Satoshi.[21] Even tech mogul Elon Musk also stands accused but denies being Satoshi Nakamoto.

---

[15] A cypherpunk is a person who is passionate about and advocates for the use of cryptographic technologies to engender digital freedom and privacy.

[16] Greenberg, A. 2014. "Nakamoto's Neighbor: My Hunt for Bitcoin's Creator Led to a Paralyzed Crypto Genius." *Forbes*, www.forbes.com/sites/andygreenberg/2014/03/25/satoshi-nakamotos-neighbor-the-bitcoin-ghostwriter-who-wasnt/?sh=69a82fa84a37 (accessed March 25, 2014).

[17] Szabo, N. 2005. "Bit Gold." *Unenumerated*, http://web.archive.org/web/20060329122942/http:/unenumerated.blogspot.com/2005/12/bit-gold.html (accessed December 29, 2005).

[18] Bigs, J. 2013. "Who Is the Real Satoshi Nakamoto? One Researcher May Have Found the Answer." *TechCrunch*, https://techcrunch.com/2013/12/05/who-is-the-real-satoshi-nakamoto-one-researcher-may-have-found-the-answer/ (accessed December 5, 2013).

[19] Szabo, N. 2007. "About Me." *Blogger*, http://web.archive.org/web/2007010908 3222/http://www.blogger.com/profile/14241889, (accessed January 9, 2007).

[20] "Smart Contracts." *ERights.org*, www.erights.org/smart-contracts/ (accessed April 25, 2021).

[21] Greenberg, A., and B. Gwern. 2015. "Is Bitcoin's Creator this Unknown Australian Genius? Probably Not (Updated)." *WIRED*, www.wired.com/2015/12/

Bitcoin is usually represented by the currency code BTC but being decentralized, and therefore not tied to a specific country, the International Standards Organization (ISO), which keeps track of internationally recognized currencies is pushing the newer abbreviation XBT for Bitcoin, in line with its rising status as a *global* medium of exchange. Under ISO, a currency not tied to a country should begin with the letter *X*.[22]

Bitcoin has varied widely in price since starting at $0.0009 on October 12, 2009 when a Finnish developer, Martti Malmi, sold 5,050 BTC[23] for $5.02.[24] One BTC remained a mere fraction of a cent until July 2010 when it rose from about $0.0008 to $0.08 in five days. It finally hit one U.S. dollar on February 9, 2011.

Bitcoin hovered around a few dollars until two years later in 2013, when it shot up, starting the year off at about $13.50 and experiencing a price rally from $80 to a peak price of $260 in early April before falling to about $70 by the middle of that month, constituting the currency's first major rally and crash. In another four years, in late 2017, Bitcoin reached a globally hailed all-time high of just under $20,000 on December 18, 2017. Prices eventually hovered under or just over $10,000 until late October 2020,[25] when a steady rise began again.

On January 29, 2021, business billionaire Elon Musk changed his Twitter bio to *#bitcoin*. In about an hour, Bitcoin's price leaped from

---

bitcoins-creator-satoshi-nakamoto-is-probably-this-unknown-australian-genius/ (accessed December 8, 2015).

[22] "Bitcoin currency code: XBT vs BTC." *Support, Kraken*, https://support. kraken.com/hc/en-us/articles/360001206766-Bitcoin-currency-code-XBT-vs-BTC (accessed April 25, 2021).

[23] Bitcoin Explorer. 2009. "Transaction Summary." *Blockchain.com*, www.blockchain.com/btc/tx/7dff938918f07619abd38e4510890396b1cef4fbeca154fb7aaf ba8843295ea2 (accessed October 12, 2009).

[24] Malmi, M. 2014. "Found the First Known Bitcoin to USD Transaction From My Email Backups. I Sold 5,050 BTC for $5,02 on 2009-10-12." *Twitter*, https://t.co/8XcBmzJljf https://twitter.com/marttimalmi/status/423455561703624704 (accessed January 15, 2014).

[25] Bitcoin price history taken from https://99bitcoins.com/bitcoin/historical-price/ and www.investopedia.com/articles/forex/121815/bitcoins-price-history. asp (accessed October 10, 2020).

about $32,000 to just under $38,000 as trading jumped from 5,000 trades per hour to about 20,000 per hour.[26] Then on February 8, 2021, Musk's company Tesla announced that it had bought $1.5 billion of Bitcoin and would begin accepting payments for its products in bitcoins.[27] Over the next few months, Bitcoin steadily rose to another all-time high of over $63,000 on April 15, 2021.[28]

The unpredictability of Bitcoin seems inherent in most cryptocurrencies at this stage as they steadily gain mainstream adoption. This volatility is expected to continue until Bitcoin and altcoins overcome regulatory hurdles and other snags to become more widely accepted; then they should stabilize and become safe alternatives to fiat currency.[29]

Delving into the crypto world can be relatively easy, depending on one's geographical location and the local regulatory regime pertaining to cryptocurrencies. A word of caution for the curious individual or investor, however; in light of Bitcoin's—and indeed all cryptocurrencies'—transient volatility at this stage of their evolution, it is advisable to inform yourself before buying and/or using your first crypto asset for any serious transaction. It may not be prudent to keep a ton of your savings in cryptocurrencies at this point. Rather, like you would treat any high-risk asset, avoid storing money that you *cannot* afford to lose. Also, guard your information and private keys, and treat your passwords with care. We will tackle how to buy, sell, and manage cryptocurrencies later in this chapter.

---

[26] Shevlin, R. 2021. "How Elon Musk Moves the Price of Bitcoin with His Twitter Activity." *Forbes*, www.forbes.com/sites/ronshevlin/2021/02/21/how-elon-musk-moves-the-price-of-bitcoin-with-his-twitter-activity/?sh=78d5ed765d27 (accessed February 21, 2021).

[27] Kovach, S. 2021. "Tesla Buys $1.5 billion in Bitcoin, Plans to Accept it as Payment." *CNBC*, www.cnbc.com/2021/02/08/tesla-buys-1point5-billion-in-bitcoin.html (accessed February 8, 2021).

[28] https://coinmarketcap.com/currencies/bitcoin/

[29] Fiat Money Is Government-Issued Currency That Is not Backed by a Physical Commodity, Such as Gold or Silver, But Rather by the Government That Issued It. Source, www.investopedia.com/terms/f/fiatmoney.asp

Ethereum and Ether (ETH)

Ether is the second most popular cryptocurrency and the number-one altcoin, with a market capitalization of about $257.67 billion.[30] Ether is the platform-specific token for all actions and transactions on the Ethereum platform and its applications. Ethereum focuses less on digital currency and more on smart contracts and hosting decentralized applications (dApps) for smartphones and other devices, making Ethereum like an alternative app marketplace, except that control of dApps remain with their creators and users rather than with mainstream intermediaries such as Apple App Store or Google Play.[31] There are over 2,782 dApps running on the Ethereum network including games, web browsers, wallets, digital marketplaces, finance apps, censorship-resistant social networks, and token exchanges.[32]

Ethereum has its own programming language that allows transactions on its network to contain executable code and not just notes, as is generally the case with Bitcoin. Additionally, ether transactions are much faster (seconds) than Bitcoin, where confirmations usually take minutes.[33] Ethereum also allows dApp developers to customize their own tokens, called ERC-20 tokens, for use as security tokens, utility tokens, or other. The ERC-20 token standard is the technical protocol for tokens built on the Ethereum blockchain, enabling compatibility and easier integration.[34] Examples of ERC-20 tokens include Basic Attention Token (BAT), OmiseGO (OMG), and Augur (REP).

---

[30] Market Capitalization Information taken from https://coinmarketcap.com (accessed April 19, 2021).

[31] "Understanding the Different Types of Cryptocurrency." *SoFi Learn*, www.sofi.com/learn/content/understanding-the-different-types-of-cryptocurrency/ (accessed January 15, 2021).

[32] "Ethereum Rankings." *State of the DApps*, www.stateofthedapps.com/platforms/ethereum (accessed April 25, 2021).

[33] Reiff, N. 2020. "Bitcoin vs. Ethereum: What's the Difference?" *Investopedia*, www.investopedia.com/articles/investing/031416/bitcoin-vs-ethereum-driven-different-purposes.asp (accessed June 16, 2020).

[34] Blockchain Support Center. 2021. "What is an ERC20 Token?" *Blockchain.com*, https://support.blockchain.com/hc/en-us/articles/360027491872-What-is-an-ERC20-token- (accessed March 31, 2021).

Ripple (XRP)

Ripple's XRP is the fourth largest cryptocurrency by market capitalization, which stands at over $62 billion at the time of writing.[35] XRP was launched in 2012 by the U.S. tech company, Ripple Labs Inc, and is a digital financial settlement system and remittance network that enables financial institutions and individuals to make real-time international payments at low costs.[36]

Unlike Bitcoin and some altcoins, Ripple's consensus mechanism does not require mining because all of its 100 billion XRP tokens were premined before launch, and this makes it speedy and reduces the energy usage and computing power required for operating on its blockchain.[37] Ripple's cross-border payment solution, RippleNet, is steadily gaining traction and has secured adoption by major banks and financial institutions in about 55 countries across six continents (at the time of writing) and the list is growing.[38]

Stablecoins

The elevated price volatility inherent in the valuation and purchasing power of Bitcoin and many altcoins, which can be deterring for crypto users, has warranted the development of *stablecoins*: unique cryptocurrencies backed by asset reserves in order to offer price stability. The resultant melding of the speedy, international portability of cryptocurrencies with the low volatilities typical of fiat currencies gives crypto users decent alternatives for safely venturing into crypto markets.

A stablecoin may attain price stability by pegging their market value to a reserve fiat currency like the U.S. dollar—these are called *fiat-collateralized stablecoins*—or to a commodity like gold or oil. They may use these reference assets as collateral or harness algorithms to buy, sell, or

---

[35] Market capitalization information taken from https://coinmarketcap.com, (accessed April 19, 2021).

[36] https://ripple.com/company

[37] https://xrpl.org/xrp.html

[38] 2021. "Real-Time Cross Border Payments for Banks." *Ripple*, https://ripple.com/use-cases/banks/ (accessed April 25, 2021).

manage these assets. Examples of fiat-collateralized stablecoins tied to the U.S. dollar are Tether (USDT), USD Coin (USDC), and TrueUSD (TUS-D).[39] Tether, which is the sixth largest cryptocurrency[40] with market capitalization of over $48 billion,[41] maintains an average token value of 1 dollar.

There are other stablecoins that are backed by reserves or portfolios of other cryptocurrencies or crypto assets. These *crypto-collateralized stablecoins* can be pegged to fiat currencies but not hold fiat reserves; rather, their reserve portfolios of crypto assets enable them to weather wild swings in cryptocurrency markets.[42] One example is Dai (DAI). Other stablecoins may not be backed by collateral reserves of fiat or crypto assets, but rather use algorithmic (or Seigniorage Supply) models to manage the supply and demand of tokens to achieve relative stability.[43] Examples of *noncollateralized* or *algorithmic stablecoins* include Ampleforth (AMPL), and Frax (FRAX).[44]

Hybrid stablecoins attempt to harness all these strategies by utilizing often-complex combinations of reserves and algorithmic models to counter volatility. An example is IDEX.[45]

Hard Forks and Soft Forks

An important concept to understand in blockchain is forking. In simple terms, a cryptocurrency is comprised of a distributed ledger containing

---

[39] Hayes, A. 2020. "Stablecoin." *Investopedia*, www.investopedia.com/terms/s/stablecoin.asp (accessed June 30, 2020).

[40] At time of writing: April 19, 2021.

[41] Market capitalization information taken from https://coinmarketcap.com (accessed October 19, 2021).

[42] 2018. "Crypto-collateralized Stablecoins." HyperQuant, https://medium.com/hyperquant/crypto-collateralized-stablecoins-129df769b089 (accessed November 11, 2018).

[43] Sam, A. 2019. "Seigniorage Supply (Algorithmic) StableCoins with 2019 Complete Guide!" https://medium.com/@alyzesam/seigniorage-supply-algorithmic-stablecoins-w-complete-list-e1c98db3b9da (accessed March 11, 2019).

[44] Bithumb Global. 2021. "Algorithmic Stablecoins: A Beginner's Guide." *Hackernoon*, https://hackernoon.com/algorithmic-stablecoins-a-beginners-guide-pmh320t (accessed January 30, 2021).

[45] Rothrie, S. 2019. "A Complete Guide to Stablecoins." *Crypto Briefing*, https://cryptobriefing.com/complete-guide-stablecoins/ (accessed December 21, 2019).

the full transactional history of the currency and this runs on a software that validates the records in the ledger. The blockchain software behind cryptocurrencies can be and are often improved, creating new versions that every node on a network will have to install. These new versions are usually backward compatible, meaning that existing tokens registered in the ledger remain valid and still run as usual on both versions of the software. In such cases, newly improved software can be thought of as mere upgrades and are called *soft forks*.

On the other hand, developers can intentionally build upon existing blockchain software and incorporate backward incompatibility, meaning that tokens on the new version cannot run on the old version. This is a *hard fork* and essentially creates a completely new token. A hard fork divides a blockchain network into two groups: one using the old version and the other using the new hard fork version with its unique token. This is how many developers have created new cryptocurrencies since the emergence of the crypto industry after Bitcoin.

Bitcoin was originally built to handle roughly seven transactions per second. Many hard forks of Bitcoin were born out of developers wanting to raise this transaction speed by increasing Bitcoin's one-megabyte block size. These include Bitcoin XT, Bitcoin Classic (BXC), and of course, Bitcoin Cash (BCH),[46] the most popular Bitcoin hard fork that has a block size of eight megabytes and a market capitalization of about $17.8 billion, making it the 10th largest cryptocurrency in the world at the time of writing.[47] Developers can also create hard forks for other reasons such as fixing security issues, reversing transactions after hack attacks, or adding new functionalities.[48]

Forks are not specific to Bitcoin and happen on other cryptocurrency networks such as Ethereum. There are countless other interesting concepts related to forking, such as metacoins and sidechains, but these are more

---

[46] Reiff, N. 2021. "A History of Bitcoin Hard Forks." *Investopedia*, www.investopedia.com/tech/history-bitcoin-hard-forks/ (accessed March 20, 2021).

[47] Market capitalization information taken from https://coinmarketcap.com (accessed April 19, 2021).

[48] Frankenfield, J. 2021. "Hard Fork (Blockchain)." *Investopedia*, www.investopedia.com/terms/h/hard-fork.asp (accessed March 4, 2021).

relevant when one gets practically involved with blockchain and acquires a modest body of experience to build upon. Expounding on them at this point will not add much usefulness to this chapter.

Buying, Exchanging, and Storing Cryptocurrency

Crypto Exchanges

Cryptocurrencies are traded on exchanges that, akin to traditional currency exchanges, serve primarily to exchange one cryptocurrency for another or for fiat currency. Generally, to buy cryptocurrency one must create an account on an exchange and then swap fiat currency for the cryptocurrency of your choice, which you can then keep in your on-platform crypto wallet or transfer to an off-platform wallet.

Credible crypto exchanges often offer three or several tiers of usability based on your level of identity verification within a Know Your Customer (KYC) framework. The basic tier usually requires nothing more than for you to set up an account using an e-mail address and a password. This will normally grant you access to funding, trade, and withdrawal functionalities with a hard limit on the quantum of cryptocurrency you can withdraw per period.

The second tier of authentication may require you to provide your full legal name, proof of address, and a government-issued ID for verification and will offer you increased funding and withdrawal limits, and other perks. The third—and usually last—tier may require financial statements and other information required for antimoney laundering (AML) verification, after which you will have full access to higher professional-level funding, trade, and withdrawal limits or unlimited features on some functionalities.

One should be careful when choosing a suitable crypto exchange because not all exchanges are as secure as they claim to be.[49] The crypto world is littered with nefarious frauds, scams, and crimes that have caused

---

[49] Frankenfield, J. 2021. "Mt. Gox." *Investopedia*, www.investopedia.com/terms/m/mt-gox.asp (accessed March 26, 2021).

billions of dollars in losses.[50] Considering the level of trust involved in signing up for an exchange account and populating it with your personal information, one has to be especially concerned with reputation and security.

One should conduct deep research into a range of prominent and niche crypto exchanges in vogue within the crypto world and consider things such as physical address, country where the exchange is based, customer support, and channels for legal redress should anything go awry. One should also inspect their range of coins and look at their transaction fees. Depending on your desired cryptocurrencies and a host of factors such as region, credibility, security, and insurance, your top choices of crypto exchanges may include Coinbase,[51] Binance,[52] Coinmama,[53] Kraken,[54] Bittrex,[55] BitOasis,[56] and Huobi.[57]

Wallets

To facilitate the easy handling of cryptocurrencies, you may take it that cryptocurrencies are stored in cryptocurrency wallets from whence they are sent and received, and that these transactions are then recorded in the blockchain's distributed ledger ... forever ... and for any and all to see, except that your identity will be masked in pseudonymity behind your unique public keys while only you hold the private keys that enable you to access the assets. But in reality, the truth is slightly different.

---

[50] Gertrude Chavez-Dreyfuss. 2020. "Cryptocurrency Crime Losses More Than Double to $4.5 Billion in 2019, Report Finds." *Reuters*, www.reuters.com/article/us-crypto-currencies-crime/cryptocurrency-crime-losses-more-than-double-to-4-5-billion-in-2019-report-finds-idUSKBN2051VT (accessed February 11, 2020).

[51] www.coinbase.com/

[52] www.binance.com/en

[53] www.coinmama.com/

[54] www.kraken.com/

[55] https://bittrex.com/

[56] https://bitoasis.net/en/home

[57] www.huobi.com/en-us/

Technically, cryptocurrency wallets do not hold actual coins and tokens, but rather they are interfaces that store your public and private keys, monitor balances, and execute transactions on the blockchain. In other words, cryptocurrencies and their transactions exist and operate on the master blockchain; thus, the operation of wallets is more of a practical system designed to enable people to use cryptocurrencies in a way that is akin to the use of regular fiat currency, making it easier to understand.

To send coins or tokens, one will need to specify a source wallet address and a destination wallet address. Each wallet has at least one address, a public key, and a private key (Figure 3.1). The address and/or public key are shareable for receiving coins while the private key is kept secret and for your eyes only. It is the combination of your private and public keys that will sanction your send or spend transactions on the blockchain. This means that with your public and private keys, anyone can access your coins and transact them on the blockchain itself. Guarding one's private keys can prevent the irreversible loss of crypto assets.

Wallets can be hot, warm, or cold: these three terms being measures of their Internet connectivity.

Figure 3.1 Example of a public address, public key, and private key

Hot Wallets

Hot wallets are set up and operated online or on Internet-enabled devices such as laptops, smartphones, and tablets. They include the complimentary wallets that come with most cryptocurrency exchanges; dedicated web wallet services; desktop wallets for laptops; and iOS, iPhone, and Android wallets for mobile devices.

Hot wallets are relatively common and easy to use but because they are online or connected to the Internet, they can hypothetically be vulnerable to attacks by online hackers; therefore, they may not be the most secure option for storing large amounts of crypto assets in the long term. In the short term, however, they give users speedy access to funds and transactions. Popular hot wallets include Bitcoin Core wallet (for Bitcoin),[58] MyEtherWallet (for Ethereum-based assets),[59] Jaxx,[60] MyCelium,[61] and Bread.[62]

Cold Wallets

Cold wallets store crypto assets offline, although they can occasionally be connected to an Internet-enabled device to receive or send coins. Cold wallets come in different forms, the most common being hardware wallets, which are electronic devices—some resembling USB flash drives—made exclusively for storing crypto assets. Some major brands of hardware wallets are Trezor (Figure 3.2),[63] Ledger (Figure 3.3),[64] CoolWallet,[65] KeepKey,[66] Ellipal,[67] and SafePal.[68] Hardware wallets are commonly secured with a pin or password and sometimes one must even push a physical button to authorize transactions. Some also come with screens for displaying and verifying contents or transactions.

Being offline, cold wallets are better than hot wallets as long-term options for storing large amounts of crypto assets. Another type of cold storage is a paper wallet. A paper wallet is made by printing—or in some cases writing—one's public key (address) and/or private key, or the mnemonic seed phrase for retrieving them. A mnemonic seed phrase is a sequence of 12 or 24 random words that can be used to recover access to

---

[58] https://bitcoin.org/en/wallets/desktop/windows/bitcoincore/
[59] www.myetherwallet.com/
[60] https://jaxx.io/
[61] https://mycelium.com/
[62] https://brd.com/
[63] https://trezor.io/
[64] www.ledger.com/
[65] www.coolwallet.io
[66] https://shapeshift.com/keepkey
[67] www.ellipal.com
[68] www.safepal.io/

Figure 3.2 Trezor One and Trezor Model T (right) Source: SatoshiLabs, Trezor Hardware Wallets

Figure 3.3 Ledger Nano X Source: Ledger

crypto assets if one loses access to a wallet or the public and private keys contained therein.

Though cold storage is generally secure from online hacking, paper wallets are still risky in other ways because they have greater likelihood for damage, loss, or physical theft. Also, paper wallets are better suited for seasoned crypto users who know what they are doing, because it is easy to write incorrect paper wallets or to miss details, which will render your funds irreversibly inaccessible or lost forever.

An innovation in paper wallets that supersedes the frailty of paper is the steel wallet. A steel wallet is a cold storage contraption built to securely bear one's mnemonic seed phrase (or public and private keys), which is etched onto its surface. Being made of stainless steel, these wallets are resistant to damage from rust, corrosion, electromagnetic pulses (EMP), and natural disasters such as fires, floods, or earthquakes. Popular steel wallet brands are Billfodl[69] and Cryptosteel.[70] Cryptotag[71] uses titanium instead of steel.

An even rarer model for cold storage is the brain wallet, which is simply the memorization of one's public and private keys or mnemonic seed phrase. A brain wallet is not for the fainthearted and is risky simply because of the possibility for one to forget.

Warm Wallets

Warm wallets normally refer to storage systems that can switch between both hot and cold wallets. These include hot wallets that incorporate some features of cold storage to engender increased security, like in some online custodian services that can be air gapped when transactions are not being made. Air gapping here means the physical or functional isolation of the wallet from the Internet and all unsecured networks, thereby turning the hot wallet into a cold storage system. True air-gapped systems are physically isolated and thus data can only be transferred through removable media, USB, network cables, firewire, and the like. For instance, some secure crypto exchanges like Liquid[72] incorporate the security of cold storage into their hot wallets so that users who do not want to manage

---

[69] https://privacypros.io/products/the-billfodl/
[70] https://cryptosteel.com/
[71] https://cryptotag.io/
[72] www.liquid.com/

cold storage themselves can sign up and have the assets in their hot wallets put into cold storage, acting like an online safety deposit box.

Choosing a Wallet

One's choice of wallet must naturally factor in their ease of accessibility, security, and the intended frequency of transactions. One can also decide to spread assets over several wallet types to reduce vulnerability to losing all assets in any one single mishap. For long-term storage, cold storage is preferable, while hot wallets are suited for short-term trades. Depending on the context, a mix of both may be prudent. Cold wallets are the most secure form of storage because they are offline and are therefore resistant to being hacked through online attacks, but they often come with the disadvantage of being pricey and capable of storing only a limited range of cryptocurrency types. But if one is going to hold a significant amount of assets, it may be worth it.

Hot wallets, being online, are the least secure form of storage but have gained prominence because they are easy to set up, are usually free or cheap, and generally accept a wider range of token types. They are also easier to access via smart devices, phones, and tablets for frequent transactions. However, their online nature makes them potentially vulnerable to technical glitches and attacks from would-be hackers.

Cryptocurrency Hygiene

Disclaimer. The numerous pieces of advice given in this chapter are not official recommendations but constitute casual guidelines to make it easier for readers to safely navigate the world of crypto. Readers should make the effort to seek advice from certified tech, cybersecurity, or legal advisers.

No financial or digital system is a hundred percent safe. Increasing security is about reducing risk to a minimum and using backup systems and contingency plans to eliminate the likelihood of losing everything.

Exclusive E-Mail Addresses

The first step to building a healthy crypto lifestyle is to create a dedicated private e-mail address (or addresses) for association with crypto-related registrations, communications, and activities. This is because crypto hackers sometimes scour the Web for publicly listed or long-lived e-mail addresses with digital footprints or trails scattered all over the Internet. Since crypto exchanges and online services require association with an e-mail account, just having your e-mail address may be sufficient for a very proficient hacker to try to compromise the *forgot password* function to reset login credentials for your wallets and then access your assets.

Set up an e-mail address that will be used exclusively for crypto assets and that will not be subscribed to all manner of newsletters, crypto news websites, and the like. Once this is done, be sure to use two-factor authentication (discussed later) as an added security measure.

Passwords—Complexity and Reuse

Be sure to use distinctive and complex passwords with lower- and upper-case alphanumeric characters and symbols. Desist from using the same password for various accounts or services.

Two-Factor Authentication (2FA)

2FA is one of the essential ways of life in the cryptocurrency universe. 2FA is the setting up of accounts and wallets to log in (or execute an action) only after a second confirmatory authentication apart from the primary username and password, hence the name, "two-factor authentication." The essence of 2FA is for websites and apps to thwart online impersonation attempts by hackers. This is achieved through the verification of secure communication with some offsite platform or device at your disposal, thereby authenticating that you are truly the bona fide user initiating the online action.

2FA can take the form of random SMS verification codes sent to your cellphone or mobile device and which you enter after your username and password to confirm that you are the real owner of the account. Unfortunately, SMS verification is a less secure type of 2FA since it is still vulnerable to SIM hacks.

The more secure and widely accepted method of 2FA is the use of dedicated authenticator apps: mainly Google Authenticator or Authy. These mobile apps iterate through six- to eight-digit, one-time-use access codes that usually refresh every minute or 30 seconds. As always, contingency planning is essential here, just as it is everywhere in the crypto world. If you use authenticator apps, be sure to save the keys or QR codes that were used to set up the authenticator, so that if the phone or device should malfunction or get lost, you can still set up the authenticator app and its accounts on a replacement device.

Some platforms also support 2FA by biometric data like fingerprints and touch ID on a phone or device. Another very secure form of 2FA is FIDO Universal 2nd Factor (U2F), which is the connection and use of USB or near-field communication (NFC) devices that a user can physically press to authenticate awareness and consent. The advantage here is that it is much simpler to push, swipe, or tap than it is to manually type in 2FA access codes. A common U2F device or solution is YubiKey.[73]

2FA is a highly effective way of ensuring that assets cannot be hacked remotely, since having your username, password, or login information will not be enough for a malicious party to compromise assets. A potential hacker would need to have physical access to your 2FA device or your biometric confirmation.

Google Fi

To mitigate the risk of SIM attacks that can compromise SMS 2FA, one can use Google Fi, which is a no-SIM mobile plan that is impossible for hackers to compromise to access your text messages and break your accounts. Currently available only in the United States, Google Fi also allows you to change your number, if you feel it is vulnerable.

---

[73] www.yubico.com/

Secure Connections and VPNs

In today's world, it can be difficult to know when someone is spying on your Internet connection. Spying can come from the unlikeliest of sources; it could be from a Wi-Fi hotspot at an airport, other users on your Wi-Fi network, or even your Internet service provider (ISP). To reduce susceptibility to attacks, avoid public networks and ensure you use secure Wi-Fi connections with strong encryption like Wireless Protected Access 2 (WPA2), especially when you are making crypto transactions.

To guard against spying and malware attacks, it is prudent to install a good antivirus solution and perform scans regularly. It is important to update devices and other software regularly so that you receive all the patches or fixes that are frequently pushed out. One may also encrypt hard drives and devices.

To secure your connection, it may be ideal to use a virtual private network (VPN). A VPN establishes a connection to a secure network that acts as an intermediary to all your online activity. A VPN will usually encrypt your connection and obscure your device's IP address and geographic location. This can shield your online activity from nosy onlookers on private or public networks. Popular VPNs include NordVPN,[74] Surfshark,[75] ExpressVPN,[76] StrongVPN,[77] and TunnelBear VPN.[78]

Online Habits

As a rule, when using crypto-related websites or whenever prompted to enter log-in credentials and sensitive information, it is a good habit to always check the web address and see if has a Secure Sockets Layer (SSL) certificate (https://), and not just http://. To avoid phishing attacks, be wary of dubious ads, e-mails, websites, and links, and avoid elaborate but shady e-mails from alleged crypto exchanges about initial coin offerings (ICOs).[79] A careful web search will often confirm the veracity or

---

[74] https://nordvpn.com/

[75] https://surfshark.com/

[76] www.expressvpn.com/

[77] https://strongvpn.com/

[78] www.tunnelbear.com/

[79] Discussed later in this chapter.

suspiciousness of such claims. When making crypto transactions, always doublecheck wallet addresses that you copy and paste, so that you will notice if malicious programs paste the wrong address instead.

Wallet Health

Where possible, generate your private keys offline when dealing with larger amounts of crypto assets and create backups of these keys as a precaution against hard drive failure, damage, or theft. Duplicate your backups and keep them in separate physical locations for insurance. Never give any person or institution your private keys under any circumstances because they are all that one needs to access your assets.

Do not keep significant funds in crypto exchanges for extended periods. Crypto assets on such exchanges should only be funds you do not mind losing. Try to separate your crypto funds into several wallets: hot wallets for short-term trades and transactions, and cold wallets for long-term storage of assets. Back up your cold storage or hardware to steel wallets for damage proof protection.

The Blockchain Economy

Now, three decades after the concept of blockchain was first proposed and almost two since Bitcoin was put forward in the whitepaper by Satoshi Nakamoto, cryptocurrencies have made amazing strides and are slowly but steadily gaining acceptance across the globe. There are at least 18,525 crypto automated teller machines (ATMs) and 275,795 other services in 72 countries, where customers can buy, sell, or exchange cryptocurrencies.[80] There are also several crypto debit card offerings in the market from platforms such as Plutus,[81] Wirex,[82] and bitpay.[83]

There are many merchants and payment gateways that now accept cryptocurrency as payment. Cryptocurrencies can now be used to

---

[80] 2021. "Bitcoin ATM Map." Coin ATM Radar, https://coinatmradar.com (accessed April 19, 2021).

[81] https://plutus.it/

[82] https://wirexapp.com/en/card

[83] https://bitpay.com/personal/

purchase products and services ranging from travel bookings, food, and groceries to real estate, cars, and luxury fashion. There are quite a few interactive merchant maps for exploring the exciting range of products and services accepting crypto around the world. A few good ones can be found on Coinmap.org, Gocrypto,[84] Bitcoinmap.cash,[85] Bitcoin.com, and on numerous other country-, merchant-, or crypto-specific sites.

Blockchain Phones

With the growing popularization of blockchain, cryptocurrencies, and decentralized applications, these technologies are beginning to make their way onto smartphones for practical, daily use. Several mainstream players in the mobile phone space have begun exploring this market by offering a few alternative phone models with blockchain or crypto wallet functionality, but these are largely just software enhancements. There is, however, at least one player whose unique product has both software and hardware features for blockchain and whose phone seems more like the shape of things to come.

Sirin Labs, one of the first entrants into this market,[86] has created the Finney blockchain smartphone.[87] The Finney phone *does* have the usual, order-qualifying, state-of-the-art technical specifications to rival other competitors; but going beyond these, it utilizes blockchain technology to offer an unprecedented level of security and has an inbuilt cold storage hardware wallet that is air gapped when not in use, but can be connected online by physically sliding it up to enable crypto transactions. The cold storage wallet has its own *safe screen*, which is revealed when slid into active mode to display your crypto assets and keys. When not in use, the wallet is slid back into place and is again air gapped, keeping your cryptocurrencies safe.

The Finney runs on Sirin OS and supports an internal crypto exchange and a host of decentralized apps (dApps) from Sirin's dCenter.

---

[84] https://gocrypto.com/en/
[85] https://bitcoinmap.cash/coinmap
[86] SIRIN LABS. 2018. "Who is SIRIN LABS?" https://medium.com/@sirin-labs/who-is-sirin-labs-1b9ffcbdb7 (accessed June 6, 2018).
[87] https://sirinlabs.com/

Other players in the smartphone market are sure to follow suit with their own concepts, opening the doors to a whole new world of blockchain smartphones and cold-wallet-embedded smart devices.

Crypto Finance: Democratizing Public Offerings and Investments

Blockchain and cryptocurrencies are making substantial impacts on the fields of investing and finance. Traditional financing options for private companies include highly regulated capital market options such as shares, stocks, bonds, and initial public offerings (IPOs). During an IPO, a company raises capital by selling stocks to the public and is then listed on a public stock exchange where its stocks can be monitored and traded. IPOs can be lengthy, heavy-duty undertakings and involve lots of scrutiny of the company and its investors by the Securities and Exchange Commission (SEC) in the United States or the relevant securities regulator in the concerned territory.

With the advent of blockchain and cryptocurrencies, new avenues have emerged for companies to gain easier access to public capital markets, and for the global public to invest in start-ups and other ventures, regardless of location. One of these crypto financing vehicles is the ICO. An ICO is the crypto equivalent of an IPO and is a process via which a venture can generate capital by selling company-specific coins, tokens, or other cryptocurrencies to investors, who in future may trade them in for cash or services when they grow in value.

A typical blockchain venture often starts with a few venture capitalist investors and grows to a stage where a proof of concept is established. With a view to scaling up, the company then settles on an ICO to raise capital from public investors. The business model and projections are then espoused in an engaging whitepaper, which is broadcast into the crypto community and pushed onto ICO listing websites such as ICO-bench,[88] NewsBTC,[89] ICO Drops,[90] ICOholder,[91] and ICObuffer.[92] This

---

[88] https://icobench.com/

[89] www.newsbtc.com/

[90] https://icodrops.com/

[91] https://icoholder.com/

[92] https://icobuffer.com/

gives people around the world an opportunity to evaluate the venture's future prospects and to buy its tokens at very cheap prices using bitcoins, major cryptocurrencies, or fiat currency.

ICOs are usually bounded by two milestones: a soft cap and a hard cap. A soft cap is the minimum amount of raised capital required to make an ICO viable, while the hard cap is the maximum amount of capital the ICO will raise. If the soft cap is not reached, the capital will be returned to the investors. Conversely, when the hard cap is reached, the ICO is completed and the business delves into full-on expansion. The company's tokens are usually then listed on crypto exchanges and can be traded at market prices. Ideally, as the business progresses, the value of its coins or tokens will rise significantly, thereby yielding decent or even substantial returns for ICO investors.

ICOs have expanded the range of financing options available to companies and increased the investing opportunities available to the global speculating public. A major benefit for a company utilizing an ICO is that it does not give away actual shares or stocks and thus retains full ownership and control of the business. Also, in most jurisdictions, there is little or no government regulation of ICOs, meaning that almost anyone can invest without having to reveal their identity or to undergo scrutiny to qualify. This is effectively democratizing the investment sector and making investing open to far-flung markets and previously excluded demographics.

It is critical to note, however, that the current lack of regulation of ICOs renders them attractive channels for scams, making them potentially dangerous. Pretty much anyone with IT savvy can create a fancy website, release a convincing whitepaper, and launch an ICO, only to vanish into the cold night when funds roll in. Many ICO tokens are ERC-20 tokens running on the Ethereum blockchain. Unfortunately, of the thousands of ERC-20 tokens in existence, most are tied to ventures that failed, have been abandoned, or were exit scams.[93]

---

[93] Wanguba, J. 2021. "How Many Cryptocurrencies Are There in 2021?" *E-Crypto News*, https://e-cryptonews.com/how-many-cryptocurrencies-are-there-in-2021/ (accessed January 28, 2021).

To safely navigate the ICO space, one must conduct due diligence on coin offerings and their management, reputation, and traceability. There are several credible websites that take the effort to thoroughly scrutinize ICOs before listing them or their whitepapers. These are good places to start, if one is looking to wade into the unpredictable, sometimes murky, waters of ICOs.

Apart from ICOs, there are other crypto financing vehicles one must be aware of.

- A **security token offering (STO)** is similar to an ICO but instead of issuing coins, a company issues tokens that are tied to underlying real-world assets like funds or to securities like stocks and bonds. With security tokens being securities, STOs fall under the purview of public securities regulators, necessitating close scrutiny of an issuing company and mandating KYC requirements, which ward off dubious investors.
- An **initial exchange offering (IEO)** is like an ICO except that rather than a company administering the ICO itself, it delegates the offering to a cryptocurrency exchange. Interested investors create accounts on the exchange and deposit funds into their wallets to trade for the IEO tokens being issued. Through an IEO, a company or project is guaranteed listing on an exchange and can leverage the existing client base of that exchange. Because exchanges perform due diligence on projects and are selective about companies they take on, IEOs are able to weed out scams, giving them an air of credibility, though in the crypto world, nothing is a hundred-percent kosher.[94]

Cryptocurrency Regulation

Cryptocurrencies were invented with the philosophy to democratize value and avoid the control of mainstream banking authorities. It is therefore

---

[94] ROKKEX. 2019. "What is the Difference Between IPO, ICO, IEO, and STO?" *The Capital*, https://medium.com/the-capital/what-is-the-difference-between-ipo-ico-ieo-and-sto-8dc6491b0db0 (accessed July 16, 2019).

no wonder that their utility and speed have caused massive worries for the financial gatekeepers whose positions and revenues are being threatened. With the unrelenting advance of cryptocurrencies, authorities have had to race to get a grip on the technology to be able to formulate their policies to regulate or streamline the crypto space.

Attempts at regulation and oversight in different regions have been varied. Some countries have decided to leave crypto alone, while others have banned cryptocurrencies outright. Some forward-thinking nations, however, have recognized that cryptocurrencies are the wave of the future and that in order to have first-mover advantage, they should rather take proactive steps to embrace the technology and integrate it into their financial systems. These are the countries that have allowed Bitcoin and crypto ATMs to flourish and have allowed payment gateways and retailers to accept crypto.

Behind all the concerns from regulatory authorities, the truth is that the fear of cryptocurrencies in many economies may probably have to do with one thing ... losing visibility of inflows into and outflows from those economies. Modern economies are not always the almighty, self-correcting equilibria that they are touted to be. During times of recessions or economic crises, it sometimes takes external interventions by financial gatekeepers to artificially sustain certain economies. Cases in point are the stimulus packages and bailouts. The timing and extent of corrective economic measures are primarily signaled by the many metrics that regulators use to monitor countrywide economic activity. These metrics are embedded in the many strict rules, regulations, and reporting mechanisms incorporated into financial transactions such as incoming and outgoing wire transfers, IPOs, import duties, income taxes, corporate taxes, and withholding taxes. Even where these protocols do not yield significant revenues for public purses, they still furnish governments with visibility on all outflows and inflows into an economy.

This is just one of many issues behind the negative attitudes of many regulators to cryptocurrencies. Indeed, the pseudonymous, decentralized, borderless, and democratic nature of cryptocurrencies could hypothetically create massive blind spots for monitoring agencies that may become oblivious to any significant capital outflows, which can stifle an economy, or to any tremendous inflows, which can spark inflation. In light of these and other concerns, crypto regulations and policy frameworks are still in evolution and it remains to be seen what equilibrium will be reached on the international stage in the long term.

CHAPTER 4

Computing, Data, and Intelligence

Contemporary breakthroughs in science and technology are making possible a whole range of unconventional computing concepts that were previously unfeasible. Enabling technologies such as miniaturization, nanotechnology, and genetic engineering are opening the doors to unusual computing paradigms that many may find surprising. This chapter explores some alternative types of computing and then delves into the field of artificial intelligence (AI).

Quantum Computing

The Dawn of Q

At its core, modern computing is built on binary code: complex combinations of ones and zeros that code into almost all of the digital data that exists today. The age of digital computing dawned with the development of metal–oxide–silicon (MOS) transistors: tiny devices made of semiconductor material which, dependent on their on or off modes, can code for the ones or zeros that form the binary foundation of our digital world.

The concept of a field-effect element was first patented in the 1920s by Julius Edgar Lilienfeld. Over the following decades, successive breakthroughs by physicists and engineers such as John Bardeen, Walter Brattain, William Shockley, Mohamed M. Atalla, and Dawon Kahng, culminated in the development of the metal–oxide–semiconductor field-effect transistor (MOSFET) at Bell Labs in 1959. Also called the metal–oxide–silicon transistor or MOS transistor, it used less power than its predecessors and was compact, making it apt for aggregation into high-density integrated circuits, also called chips or microchips.

Subsequent improvements by companies such as Fairchild Semiconductor, RCA, Intel, General Microelectronics (GMe), IBM, Philips, and Micron, continually made transistors smaller and more efficient, fueling the explosion in computing power that ushered mankind into the digital age.[1] The MOS transistor is now the most produced device in history, with billions produced every day.[2]

Gordon E. Moore—cofounder of Fairchild Semiconductor and Intel—postulated in 1965 that the density of integrated circuits would double, while costs would halve, every year for a decade.[3] But in 1975, as MOS transistors continued to shrink, he renewed his growth prediction but with doubling every two years.[4] *Moore's law* has stayed true beyond its original timelines to the present day where typical transistors are between 10 and 20 nanometers, just tens of atoms thick,[5] and are fast approaching five nanometers, which is considered the hard minimum for conventional silicon transistors.[6]

Approaching the end of the atomic scale places a theoretical limit on the expansion of traditional transistor technology, while demand

---

[1] David, L. 2018. "13 Sextillion & Counting: The Long & Winding Road to the Most Frequently Manufactured Human Artifact in History." *CHM Blog*, https://computerhistory.org/blog/13-sextillion-counting-the-long-winding-road-to-the-most-frequently-manufactured-human-artifact-in-history/ (accessed April 2, 2018).

[2] David, L. 2013. "Who Invented the Transistor?" *CHM Blog*, https://computerhistory.org/blog/who-invented-the-transistor/?key=who-invented-the-transistor (accessed December 4, 2013).

[3] Moore, G.E. 1965. "Cramming More Components Onto Integrated Circuits." *Electronics* 38, no. 8, p. 114.

[4] Simonite, T. 2016. "Moore's Law Is Dead. Now What?" *MIT Technology Review*, www.technologyreview.com/2016/05/13/245938/moores-law-is-dead-now-what/ (accessed May 13, 2016).

[5] Thompson, A. 2016. "Scientists Have Made Transistors Smaller Than We Thought Possible." *Popular Mechanics*, www.popularmechanics.com/technology/a23353/1nm-transistor-gate/ (accessed October 12, 2016).

[6] Desai, S.B., S.R. Madhvapathy, A.B. Sachid, J.P. Llinas, Q. Wang, G.H. Ahn, . . . and A. Javey. October 2016. "MoS2 Transistors With 1-Nanometer Gate Lengths." *Science (New York, N.Y.)* 354, no. 6308, 99–102. https://doi.org/10.1126/science.aah4698

for computing power continues to skyrocket[7] as we enter the Fourth Industrial Revolution. This dilemma has led computer scientists to look beyond classical physics and into the quantum realm for solutions that could power the next generation of computers.

The Science Behind Quantum Computing

Conventional computing has the basic unit of a *bit*, which can code for zero or one. For quantum computing, computer scientists have crafted the *qubit* (quantum bit), a basic unit suitable for interpreting the mechanics of quantum superposition, quantum entanglement, and quantum interference into data.[8]

Quantum superposition occurs when certain particles simultaneously exist in either of two states, neither of them, both of them, or a superposition of all of the states in between; and allows a qubit to code for not just zero or one, but for both, everything in between, or any proportion of the two states. This drastically expands the spectrum of data that a qubit can grasp, compared to a classical bit, and allows unprecedent processing power. For example, five classical bits can have one configuration at a time out of 32 (or 2^5) possible arrangements, whereas in quantum computing, five qubits in superposition can be in all 32 configurations at once. As more qubits are added, the number of configurations grows exponentially.

Quantum entanglement is a key feature of quantum mechanics whereby certain pairs or groups of particles exhibit a special connection such that the state of one particle affects or reflects the state of the other(s) even when they are far apart. This allows two entangled qubits to react instantaneously to changes in each other's state, regardless of the distance

---

[7] Wang, D., and C. Jared. 2018. "Computing Faces an Energy Crunch Unless New Technologies are Found." *The Conversation*, https://theconversation.com/computing-faces-an-energy-crunch-unless-new-technologies-are-found-106060 (accessed November 28, 2018).

[8] "What is Quantum Computing?" *IBM*, www.ibm.com/quantum-computing/learn/what-is-quantum-computing/ (accessed April 25, 2021).

between them; therefore, by measuring the state of one, we can deduce the state of the other.

Quantum interference happens when particles act as waves and interact with each other such that their amplitudes superpose and result in a blended wave, which can have higher amplitude (constructive) or lower amplitude (destructive), depending on the frequencies of the individual waves and to what extent they are in or out of phase. Quantum interference allows qubits to not just be in several states at once but to also vary in amplitude, akin to brightness or intensity. This signal strength adds another dimension to the data that qubits can hold.

The Quantum Race

To be truly revolutionary, a functioning quantum computer may have to demonstrate quantum supremacy, which is the ability to perform mathematical calculations far beyond the capabilities of contemporary, classical supercomputers.[9] This is no longer a theoretical plausibility, but a reality; quantum computers exist, mostly as early-stage demonstration models, but are already being tested in public and private domains, so that the science progresses in tandem with business development. What follows is an overview of some key highlights in the history of quantum computing.

In 1998 in the United States, Isaac Chuang, Neil Gershenfeld, and Mark Kubinec built a 2-qubit computer that demonstrated the principles of quantum computing but just for a few nanoseconds. Then, in March 2000, a 7-qubit quantum computer using trans-crotonic acid was built by Emanuel Knill, Raymond Laflamme, and Rudy Martinez of Los Alamos National Laboratory and Ching-Hua Tseng of the Massachusetts Institute of Technology (MIT).[10]

Google started looking at quantum computing in 2006, and in 2012, it launched its Quantum Artificial Intelligence lab (QuAIL) in Goleta, a

---

[9] Giles, M. 2019. "Explainer: What is a Quantum Computer?" *IT Technology Review*, www.technologyreview.com/2019/01/29/66141/what-is-quantum-computing/ (accessed January 29, 2019).

[10] Holton, W.C. 2020. "Quantum Computer." *Encyclopedia Britannica*, www.britannica.com/technology/quantum-computer (accessed August 16, 2020).

city in Santa Barbara County, California. In 2018, the company released a record-breaking 72-qubit processor called Bristlecone, yet the team at QuAIL had also been working on an alternative chip with fewer qubits but that could likely perform better, and this gained more traction.[11] Then in October 2019, Google announced that its 53-qubit quantum processor, *Sycamore*, had achieved quantum supremacy by solving a complex calculation in 200 seconds that would otherwise have taken the world's most powerful supercomputer at that time—the IBM-built *Summit*—a few days or up to 10,000 years to solve.[12]

IBM, one of Google's leading rivals in quantum development, is also at the cutting edge of the science, but is chasing more than just quantum supremacy; it seeks *quantum advantage*, a concept that focuses more on relevance and applicability to real-world challenges. IBM is running technical R&D in tandem with business development activities that explore practical applications of the technology to industry and individuals. This is being done through the *IBM Q Experience*,[13] which was launched in 2016 to give third parties access to IBM's quantum computers through the cloud. As of February 2020, the program had 15 5- to 53-qubit quantum computers available to clients and the public, and which are accessed by about 12,000 people per month, including kids.

Through IBM Q Experience, the company is gaining direct insights from the market about probable uses for the technology and ideas for shaping software, applications, and interfaces to facilitate smooth user experiences. Concurrently, IBMers are also able to analyze the viability of the business prospects of quantum computing. IBM believes that this integrated, customer-centric approach to innovation is a better path to

---

[11] Lichfield, G. 2020. "Inside the Race to Build the Best Quantum Computer on Earth." *MIT Technology Review*, www.technologyreview.com/2020/02/26/916744/quantum-computer-race-ibm-google/ (accessed February 26, 2020).

[12] Childers, T. 2019. "Google's Quantum Computer Just Aced an 'Impossible' Test." *Live Science*, www.livescience.com/google-hits-quantum-supremacy.html (accessed October 24, 2019).

[13] https://quantum-computing.ibm.com/

securing competitive quantum advantage.[14] This may hold some merit, because Google has also started collaborating with third-party users to experiment with its quantum technologies. Clients include Daimler, U.S. Department of Energy (DOE), and Volkswagen.

Another important company in quantum circles is D-Wave Systems, Inc. which was founded in 1999 and is headquartered in Burnaby, British Columbia, in Canada. D-Wave stands out as the first supplier of commercial quantum computers in the world, although the workings of its quantum technologies differ from other quantum processors by the likes of Google and IBM.

D-Wave released its first offering, the 128-qubit *D-Wave One*, in 2011 with a price tag of $10 million. Unlike other quantum computers, D-Wave One uses superconducting loops and magnetic fields to harness the phenomenon of *quantum annealing*. This unique approach to quantum computing allows its integrated circuits to be built similarly to MOS circuits; hence, they can be programmed with some conventional programming languages. The downside of D-Wave One was that it was designed to tackle a specific type of task: discrete optimization problems. Regardless, D-Wave quickly secured a contract with Lockheed Martin and since then has had a long list of other clients including some of the world's most advanced organizations, including NASA Ames, Volkswagen, Universities Space Research Association (USRA), DENSO, Los Alamos National Laboratory USC, Oak Ridge National Laboratory. In fact, D-Wave provided the first quantum computers at Google Quantum AI lab, before Google developed their own.[15]

D-Wave has strong ties with the University of British Columbia because of its founders and has built an impressive record of strategic partnerships with leading quantum research efforts in universities across the world and institutions like NASA's Jet Propulsion Laboratory. The company has over 160 U.S. patents and publishes heavily in top industry journals. The company's latest offering is the 5,000-qubit Advantage

---

[14] Lichfield, G. n.d. "Inside the race to Build the Best Quantum Computer on Earth."

[15] "Meet D-Wave." *D-Wave*, www.dwavesys.com/our-company/meet-d-wave (accessed April 25, 2021).

quantum system that has 15-way qubit connectivity and is available to customers through a quantum cloud service called Leap. D-Wave Advantage is tailored more toward businesses and allows the crafting of hybrid quantum applications for its client companies such as Volkswagen, Save-On-Foods, Accenture, and Menten AI.[16]

Another player in the quantum race is Honeywell. In June 2020, Honeywell announced that its quantum computer, *H0*, had achieved 64 on a metric called *quantum volume*, which, simply put, is a function of number of qubits, processing power, and efficiency. This claim supposedly made H0 the world's fastest quantum computer at the time, with twice the performance of its closest rivals. Honeywell is hoping to make waves in the quantum industry and has partnered with Microsoft to use its Azure Quantum platform to boost the access of organizations to quantum computing.[17]

In December 2020, Chinese scientists from the University of Science and Technology of China (USTC) in Shanghai outdoored their own quantum computer, *Jiuzhang*, which runs on photons, claiming the title of the world's fastest quantum computer.[18] This unique light-based machine that uses lasers, mirrors, prisms, and optical circuits, demonstrated quantum primacy (a better term for quantum supremacy[19]) and was able to perform a specific Gaussian boson sampling (GBS) task a hundred trillion times faster than the best classical supercomputers.[20]

---

[16] "D-Wave Announces General Availability of First Quantum Computer Built for Business." D-Wave, www.dwavesys.com/press-releases/d-wave-announces-general-availability-first-quantum-computer-built-business (accessed September 29, 2020).

[17] "The World's Highest Performing Quantum Computer is Here." *Honeywell*, www.honeywell.com/us/en/news/2020/06/the-worlds-highest-performing-quantum-computer-is-here (accessed April 25, 2021).

[18] Letzter, R. 2020. "China Claims Fastest Quantum Computer in the World." www.livescience.com/china-quantum-supremacy.html (accessed December 7, 2020).

[19] Durham, I., G. Daniel, and W. Karoline. 2021. "Physicists Need to Be More Careful With How They Name Things." *Scientific American*, www.scientificamerican.com/article/physicists-need-to-be-more-careful-with-how-they-name-things/ (accessed February 20, 2021).

[20] Daniel, G. 2020. "Light-Based Quantum Computer Exceeds Fastest Classical Supercomputers." *Scientific American*, www.scientificamerican.com/article/light-based-quantum-computer-exceeds-fastest-classical-supercomputers/ (accessed December 3, 2020).

The quantum revolution is truly on and many companies are racing to get in on the action. There are many other players in this race that I did not detail for lack of space and they include IonQ,[21] Intel, Rigetti Computing,[22] Quantum Circuits,[23] and even Amazon. With so many companies jumping on the quantum bandwagon, many stakeholders are optimistic about the future of the quantum computing market. Some analysts predict spending on quantum technology to reach $9.1 billion by 2030,[24] while other researchers anticipate the overall quantum computing market in 2030 to surpass $64 billion.[25]

Applications

Quantum computing holds promise for an amazing array of applications. It is reasonable to expect the quantum revolution to permeate into any niche currently occupied by classical computing. An obvious, future use of quantum computing would be for scientific research. Quantum computing could facilitate the improved simulation of quantum phenomena, atomic structures, molecules, and physical laws. Using quantum technology, researchers will be able to accurately test quantum theories and perform experiments. Quantum technology is already being explored by the European Organization for Nuclear Research (CERN) to improve data analyses in future particle physics experiments.[26]

---

[21] https://ionq.com/

[22] www.rigetti.com/

[23] https://quantumcircuits.com/

[24] Reichert, C. 2020. "Amazon, IBM and Microsoft Race to Bring Global Access to Quantum Computing." *CNET*, www.cnet.com/news/amazon-ibm-and-microsoft-race-to-bring-global-access-to-quantum-computing/ (accessed April 29, 2020).

[25] "Quantum Computing Market Size – Superpositioned for Growth?" *The Quantum Daily*, https://thequantumdaily.com/2020/02/18/the-quantum-computing-market-size-superpositioned-for-growth/ (accessed February 18, 2020).

[26] Chalmers, M. 2020. "CERN Meets Quantum Technology." *CERN*, https://home.cern/news/news/computing/cern-meets-quantum-technology (accessed September 30, 2020).

Quantum computing is expected to enable the simulation of matter with unprecedented accuracy, and this has the potential to trigger extensive advances in the field of materials science that will enhance the production of lighter, stronger, and more efficient materials for vehicle structures, machine parts, frames, solar panels, and electronic devices. Of course, another major application could be the development of higher-capacity batteries for electric cars, space rovers, and all electric forms of mobility.

The simulation of matter is especially relevant to medicine and the pharmaceutical industry. Quantum computing applications could help model complex molecules or compounds in research efforts aimed at developing active ingredients for new, more effective drugs. The precise simulation of protein structures will allow a better understanding of how proteins interact and fold, and therefore help in modeling drug interactions with body tissues, before clinical trials on living subjects.

A noteworthy capability of quantum computing is optimization. Quantum computers can analyze vast amounts of data and generate optimal solution sets and forecasts at fantastic speeds. Optimization and forecasting functions are extremely useful in flow optimization and hence could be valuable for improving navigation in the various mobility sectors. Quantum computing could help optimize traffic flows in aviation, road transport, and shipping; and could deduce more rapid or energy-saving routes for navigation.

The pattern-recognition functions of quantum computers could be used to analyze enormous amounts of medical data to identify risk factors and boost preventative health care so that diseases are intercepted earlier. Likewise, these forecasting capabilities are expected to become invaluable in polling and the modeling or forecasting of elections. They could also be used to analyze massive climate data and model more accurate weather forecasts. The ability to perform speedy searches of unimaginably large databases will be of utmost importance to security agencies such as police, immigration, and intelligence outfits that are having to manage stunning amounts of big data in ever-growing repositories of surveillance and transactional data.

Obviously, the optimization and forecasting capabilities of quantum computers will be invaluable to business and financial sectors. Q apps could be utilized to manage financial big data, analyze financial risk, detect fraud, and optimize trading strategies. The technology could speed up and finetune accurate credit scoring. Quantum computing could help optimize the performance of business functions such as supply chain logistics, workforce management, operations management, and process automation in manufacturing, all leading to cost reductions and marked performance improvements.

One prospective application of quantum computing that many computer scientists look forward to is in the advancement of AI. Lightning-fast pattern recognition and speedy analysis of immense data sets are perfectly suited for machine learning and could speed up progress in the development of functional AI solutions. Similarly, quantum computing could make impacts on the gaming world and allow the precise recreation of natural laws in virtual environments within virtual reality (VR) and augmented reality (AR) applications for games or design industries such as automotive and architectural design.

Possible Threats and Challenges

While quantum computing may revolutionize the digital world in a positive way, there are still threats that could arise from the commercial adoption of the technology. Chief among these is security. The ease of quantum computing to handle cryptographic algorithms at unprecedented speeds makes it a source of both worry and relief to cybersecurity and regulatory entities. It is certain that quantum computers will be able to break the codes unpinning Rivest-Shamir-Adleman (RSA) encryption and other cryptographic systems that support conventional secure communications. This poses a danger from hackers and cyberterrorists, especially in our current geopolitical climate where cyberwarfare is a reality. Damages from quantum-enabled cyberattacks could range from financial theft to misinformation, election fraud, systems sabotage, and hacks of intelligence agencies. This is the bad news.

The good news, ironically, is that while they may be good at cracking classical encryption, quantum computers could be just as adept at generating and testing quantum-resistant cryptography, which is expected to be potentially unhackable. Classic encryption techniques are based on mathematical algorithms and thus can be cracked if enough computing power is available, although the immense processing power required to crack some of these complex codes makes it largely unfeasible for classic computers. Quantum encryption, however, would be based on the fundamental laws of physics, which cannot be broken, making quantum encryption hypothetically unbreakable. It is not possible to precisely copy quantum information since it is probabilistic, thus making it impossible to copy quantum encryption keys, regardless of the quantum resources available.

The implication of these facts is that digital infrastructure around the globe will have to be upgraded to become quantum-resistant before quantum computers are set loose on the world stage in the near future. Especially pertinent would be the quantum proofing of financial, governmental, and intelligence communications from quantum cyber-attacks.

Another set of challenges centers on the building of quantum computers themselves. The quantum phenomena that form the basis of quantum computing are so minute and delicate that currently, they only last for a twinkle of a second, after which they decohere. Decoherence is a limiting factor on current quantum computers, which strive to sustain coherence time and quantum superstition or entanglement for as long as possible while they execute calculations. Some of Google's quantum chips cohere for only 30 to 40 microseconds, while some other chips by IBM can reach up to 500 microseconds although they process less quantum gates.[27]

Also, the quantum signals can easily be disturbed by external energies, particles, and heat. Therefore, these qubits have to be protected from the environment's electronic, magnetic, and heat energies, otherwise it becomes like trying to listen to a piano concerto while standing next to the jet engine of an aircraft. To do this, qubits are usually chilled to as close to absolute zero as possible, usually 0.015 to 0.1 Kelvin (−273.135 to −273.05 degrees Celsius),[28] which is even colder than the average

---

[27] Lichfield, G. n.d. "Inside the Race to Build the Best Quantum Computer on Earth."

[28] Krewell, K. and Tirias Research. 2018. "Does IBM Have the Quantum Advantage?" *Forbes*, www.forbes.com/sites/tiriasresearch/2018/09/18/does-ibm-have-the-quantum-advantage/?sh=6d7327ae54e8 (accessed September 18, 2018).

temperature of outer space (283.32 Kelvin or 10.17 degrees Celsius) or interstellar space (3 Kelvin or -270.15 degrees Celsius).[29] Such low temperatures eliminate outside energies from disturbing the qubits and causing errors in calculations.[30]

Cooling requirements and the tendency to decohere place serious constraints on computer engineers and are costly to mitigate, thus quantum computers are currently incredibly expensive. Some computer scientists are working to create quantum systems where qubits can pass on their calculations to neighboring qubits as they decohere, resulting in a continuous relay race of processing power, which will cycle through a large number of qubits. This is just one of many possible strategies for creating fault-tolerant quantum systems.[31]

Another major consideration for the future of quantum technology is software development. There is a growing realization that binary computing may not be sufficient to utilize the full potential of qubits, which can code for more than just ones and zeros. Some scientists are beginning to toy with the plausibility of ternary, quaternary, and even five-state computing models as better alternatives for building software that can harness the amazing data range of qubits in quantum computers.[32] Meanwhile, a handful of companies are speedily developing quantum software that will run the hardware when it becomes main stream. Microsoft is aware of the big impact quantum computing could make and has released its domain-specific *Q#* (Q sharp) programming language, which is designed for handling quantum algorithms.

---

[29] Libal, A. 2018. "The Temperatures of Outer Space Around the Earth." *Sciencing*, https://sciencing.com/temperatures-outer-space-around-earth-20254.html (accessed April 13, 2018).

[30] Reichert, C. n.d. "Amazon, IBM and Microsoft Race to Bring Global Access to Quantum Computing." CNET.

[31] Lichfield, G. n.d. "Inside the race to Build the Best Quantum Computer on Earth."

[32] Marks, P. 2009. "Ditching Binary Will Make Quantum Computers More Powerful." *NewScientist*, www.newscientist.com/article/dn17575-ditching-binary-will-make-quantum-computers-more-powerful/ (accessed August 10, 2009).

How to Prepare

The onslaught of quantum computing is almost certain and is sure to ripple through the business world. It may be wise to prepare or at least start evaluating the impacts it can have on your industry. For the business professional interested in adding quantum-computing credentials to their profile, there are a many free or paid courses, certifications, and immersions available to get you playing with the world of Q now.

For starters, one can get involved in some of the quantum initiatives previously mentioned in this chapter, like IBM's Q Experience[33] and D-Wave's Leap.[34] One can also explore educational resources on Google's Quantum AI[35] and several courses on LinkedIn Learning.[36]

Cloud Computing

The advent of personal computing launched a paradigm of users possessing their data at home or in the office, and when necessary, having to transport the data about by carrying it on physical floppy disks, compact disks, and removable media. The arrival of the Internet changed this dynamic by enabling data to be transported electronically between users, and facilitated the development of cloud computing, which is transforming not only how data is moved around but also where the data lives.

Cloud computing is the assignment of data storage, processing, and other digital assets to remote servers and networks, which could be private or third party. While many large companies operate their own private clouds for the purpose of proprietary integrity and security, a growing number are beginning to trust big-name, dedicated cloud players with solid reputations. Cloud computing can be impactful on businesses by saving them the heavy investments in equipment and expertise necessary to build functional computer networks and servers in-house. Outsourcing

---

[33] https://quantum-computing.ibm.com/

[34] https://cloud.dwavesys.com/leap/signup/

[35] https://quantumai.google/education

[36] www.linkedin.com/learning/search?keywords=quantum%20computing

large proportions of computing needs to competent third parties frees companies to focus more on their businesses and less on tech logistics.

The cloud outsourcing model is still evolving. Some established players and niche competitors have already added supply chain and inventory management to their offerings and are exploring other services to snatch from the domain of traditional businesses. Prices for cloud services keep plummeting, further strengthening the commercial rationale for the increased adoption of cloud services on an unprecedented scale.

Contemporary cloud services can be grouped into several categories, the main ones being IaaS, PaaS, FaaS, and SaaS.[37] Infrastructure as a Service (IaaS) is a cloud model dedicated to more rudimentary, hardware-related computing needs such as processing power, data storage, and sometimes, network resources.

Platform as a Service (PaaS) or application platform as a service (aPaaS) focuses more on providing specialized platforms or toolkits to skilled developers who use them to build and deploy digital applications for their own clients. This saves specialist developers the headache and expense of building locally those resources that have the likelihood to be underutilized. PaaS packages can include state-of-the-art development tools, programming languages and libraries, all offered securely on a per-use basis. Function as a service (FaaS) is similar to PaaS or aPaaS, except that it is a utility computing model based more on functionality charged on an on-demand basis. FaaS is sometimes called serverless and this is discussed further later in the next section.

Through Software as a Service (SaaS), cloud companies host and manage software or applications and grant access to business-to-business (b2b) or business-to-consumer (b2c) clients through desktop browsers or mobile apps. This allows clients to focus on using the apps instead of getting caught up in software development, updates, bug fixes, or hiring specialist staff. SaaS packages typically include e-mail services, data storage, and more.

---

[37] "The Ultimate Business Owner's Guide to Information Technology." *EOX Technology Solutions*, www.eoxtechnologysolutions.com/business-owners-guide-to-it (accessed April 24, 2021).

The outsourcing of infrastructure, platform, function, and software services fosters many advantages for cloud companies and their clients. Cloud companies are able to leverage economies of scale to reduce per-service costs for clients and are able to build institutional expertise in critical areas like cybersecurity, giving clients increased confidence that their digital assets are protected by the state-of-the-art reliability. Conversely, client companies are able to reduce the sizes of their IT teams, reduce payroll, and preclude high maintenance costs.

What Is Serverless Computing?

Serverless computing, often analogous to Function as a Service (FaaS), is a popular concept in tech circles that can be confusing or hard to distinguish in parlance from regular cloud computing. In fact, a lot of the cloud computing features described in the previous section fall under serverless architecture. The truth is that the lines are quite blurred. Serverless computing can sometimes be thought of as another model within cloud computing.

Strictly speaking, serverless computing refers to any category of computing as a service that is run on host servers. In common tech usage, however, the term serverless usually refers to third-party cloud servers that allocate variable resources to your site or apps based on demand. Traditional cloud solutions may offer tiered quanta of resources, regardless of whether they are sufficiently used or underutilized, thereby nudging clients to opt for superior packages in order to cope with peaks in usage, even if they occur only infrequently. Serverless architecture, however, dedicates the precise units of resources needed to match the fluctuating demands of your apps or sites in real time. This is called automatic scaling or auto-scaling. Thus, whereas normal cloud services may charge fixed rates per package per period, serverless costs are elastic and vary to adapt to your demand profile.[38] Through the serverless model, therefore, clients

---

[38] Gladu, B. 2018. "What's the Difference Between Cloud Computing and Serverless?" *NorthStack*, https://northstack.com/cloud-computing-vs-serverless/ (accessed October 26, 2018).

can avoid paying for formidable computing-as-a-service capabilities, which may be underutilized during off-peak periods.

It is important to note that being serverless only refers to a lack of servers on the client side of things; there are indeed server architecture and hardware powering the service, but their setup, operation, and maintenance rest exclusively in the provider's domain.

Cloud Access Models

Businesses can leverage cloud technologies via several models. Many cloud providers operate a *public cloud* model to make data storage space and applications available to customers over the Internet through web or mobile applications on a subscription, pay-as-you-go, or per-use basis. However, businesses concerned with intellectual property and security can opt for the *private cloud* model, which is typically more expensive to build and staff, but allows them to maintain control over their software and digital assets, and to control access protocols. This ensures intellectual property and competitive advantage is protected.

Businesses can also employ a *hybrid cloud* model to allocate certain digital assets to public clouds while maintaining critical or sensitive assets on their private clouds. Another tier is the *community cloud* model, where cloud services are harnessed by an umbrella of customers or organizations. Community clouds can be privately built by a community or hosted by a public third party, or a hybrid of these.

The Cloud Market

Currently (at the time of writing), the cloud market is dominated by two big players, with Amazon Web Services (AWS) in pole position holding 33 percent of global market share in the fourth quarter of 2020,[39] followed by Microsoft Azure, holding 20 percent. Other big players in the market include Google, IBM, Alibaba, VMWare by Dell, and Oracle.

---

[39] "Global Quarterly Market Share of Cloud Infrastructure Services from 2017 to 2020, by Vendor." *Statista*, www.statista.com/statistics/477277/cloud-infrastructure-services-market-share/ (accessed April 25, 2021).

These big-name cloud providers draw in equally big-name cloud clients. Apple, for instance, maintains its cloud-based services like iCloud and Apple Music using a mix of its own cloud division—*Apple Cloud Infrastructure (ACI)*—and AWS to which some say it may be paying up to $30 million monthly, as well as Google Cloud.[40] Other reputable cloud subscribers include Netflix, Airbnb, Xerox, and Pinterest.[41]

Yet, apart from AWS and other big cloud companies, a host of smaller players are gaining ground by carving out niche portfolios for specialized chunks of the market. Some do this by offering customized support to b2b companies that specialize in advanced software tools, and by targeting start-ups seeking cheaper solutions.[42] Current examples are Rackspace, DigitalOcean, Virtustream, IONOS, Pax8, and the French company OVH's American subsidiary, OVH US, which acquired vCloud Air from VMWare in 2019. Some of these smaller players also attract big names who need cloud services but whose product offerings are in direct competition with rival offerings by some big cloud players themselves, such as Amazon and Google who also deal in e-mail, video streaming, and music. By sticking to bespoke cloud services, niche cloud providers preclude potential conflicts of interest that may ward off future clients. Other small players distinguish themselves by offering a unique mix of managed services such as supply chain management, marketing, and media.

Clouds on the Horizon

With the growing adoption of cloud services, the nature of the technologies and product offerings continue to evolve. Many companies are using the *multicloud* approach of spreading assets between two or more cloud

---

[40] Taarini, K.D. 2020. "Is Apple Planning to Enter Cloud Computing Space?" *Forbes*, www.forbes.com/sites/taarinikaurdang/2020/05/31/is-apple-planning-to-enter-cloud-computing-space/?sh=46f1267c2d53 (accessed May 31, 2020).

[41] GilAllouche. 2018. "7 Well-Known Companies Who Have Moved to the Cloud." *SmartData Collective*, www.smartdatacollective.com/7-well-known-companies-have-moved-cloud/ (accessed April 25, 2021).

[42] Melendez, S. 2018. "Amid the Cloud Giants, Small Providers Find their Niche." *Fast Company*, www.fastcompany.com/40561868/amid-the-cloud-giants-small-providers-find-their-niche (accessed May 21, 2018).

providers; however, this is quickly morphing into an *omni-cloud* approach where clients spread different assets across many major, small, and niche cloud providers to be able to leverage the best features in the market. This is helped by the fact that there is a general industry drive toward compatibility and standardization in public, on-premises, and hosted private cloud infrastructure.[43]

Another unstoppable trend is the infiltration of AI into cloud service offerings. Artificial Intelligence as a Service (AIaaS), where users can harness AI capabilities via cloud platforms, is gaining steady popularity, being cheaper and less risky than building those capabilities in-house. As more AI functionalities materialize, they are likely to first reach the public through their steady percolation into cloud service offerings.

Cloud Learning and Development

The world of cloud computing is jam-packed with a dizzying plethora of industry jargons and, for the uninitiated, the learning curve can be steep. They include things such as kubernetes, backend as a service (BaaS), AWS Lambda, Amazon Fargate, containers, pods, microservice architecture, application programming interfaces (APIs), and multitenancy. But with the growing ease of subscribing to and using cloud services, investing heavily in learning the nitty-gritty of the technology may not engender significant marginal benefits to one's use of the services, depending on one's role. However, it is still empowering to gain and exhibit understanding of the cloud space.

To this end, I would recommend the many courses and learning paths on LinkedIn Learning for studying cloud fundamentals or for preparing for the myriad of cloud certifications.[44] For those seeking industry-standard certifications for their resumes, there exist several reputable courses taught at credible institutions, including the comprehensive

---

[43] Tsidulko, J. 2019. "10 Emerging Cloud Computing Trends to Watch in 2020." www.crn.com/news/cloud/10-emerging-cloud-computing-trends-to-watch-in-2020 (accessed November 14, 2019).

[44] www.linkedin.com/learning/search?keywords=cloud

six-month Post Graduate Program in Cloud Computing[45] offered online by Great Learning and McCombs School of Business, of the University of Texas, Austin. Simplilearn and Caltech's Center for Technology and Management Education (Caltech CTME) also offer their own Post Graduate Program in Cloud Computing, a course designed to develop cloud experts proficient in Azure, AWS, GCP, and architectural principles.[46] And there are many more.

Optical Computing

Classical computers are built upon electrical architecture and thus computation speeds are limited by the speed of electrons and the conductive resistance of metallic components. Computer scientists are currently experimenting with alternative infrastructure, which may allow computations to run on photons, which are faster, traveling at the speed of light.[47]

The suitability of light for rapid data transmission is well known because of its use in fiberoptic technology, which serves as the backbone of modern, high-speed intra- and intercontinental telecommunications. Optical, light, or photonic computing brings this technology into the domain of computer processing.

To rival the MOS transistors of electronic computers, optical computers will require optical transistors or processors and some form of optical data transfer, most likely using fiberoptics. Finally, optical computers may require optical storage.

There are two main schools or eventualities in the field of optical computing: pure optical computers and electro-optical hybrid computers. Pure optical computers are constructed exclusively on optical infrastructure running on waves, pulses, or packets of light of multiple frequencies, and are devoid of electron-based systems. Electro-optical hybrid

---

[45] www.mygreatlearning.com/us/cloud-computing/courses/pg-program-online-cloud-computing-course?arz=1

[46] www.simplilearn.com/pgp-cloud-computing-certification-training-course

[47] Dunietz, J. 2017. "Light-Powered Computers Brighten AI's Future." *Scientific American*, www.scientificamerican.com/article/light-powered-computers-brighten-ai-rsquo-s-future/ (accessed June 30, 2017).

computers blend optical components with classic silicon or electronic infrastructure but the several conversions between binary code and light pulses during transmission introduce energy losses into the system, about 30 percent per conversion.[48] These constitute severe limitations on the feasibility of hybrid electro-optical computer systems.

But while all-optical computers offer the alluring possibility of seamless, lossless optical data transmission, there are a few challenges to overcome. These pure optical systems will require a full complement of optical counterparts to traditional electronic components; these will include optical processors, optical transistors, optical logic gates, optical switches, optical fibers, lens arrays, lasers, and optical or holographic memory.

Despite these hurdles, the prospect of optical computers holds much promise. Optical computers will be smaller and faster. They will use extraordinarily little power with very little transmission losses, and this has beneficial consequences on their energy footprint. Their low power consumption and speed will make them ideal for AI applications. Their reliance on light also makes them immune to disturbances from the external environment such as radio frequencies or electromagnetic interference.

The Photonics Market

The race to enter and dominate the photonic computing market is led by a host of start-ups, which often collaborate or compete with research departments of more established tech firms. The UK-based company, Optalysys, launched a first-of-its-kind optical coprocessor, the FT:X2000, in 2019.[49] The company is focused on innovating speedy optical systems with low energy consumption for use in AI, especially deep learning and pattern recognition. The company is gaining traction and has already collaborated on projects with the U.S. Defense Advanced Research Projects

---

[48] David, D. 2001. *Nolte, Mind at Light Speed: A New Kind of Intelligence*, 34. NY: Simon and Schuster, The Free Press.
[49] Feldman, M. 2019. "Startup Sheds Some Light on Optical Processing." *The Next Platform*, www.nextplatform.com/2019/03/11/startup-sheds-some-light-on-optical-processing (accessed March 11, 2019).

Agency (DARPA), the Earlham Institute, and the European Centre for Medium-Range Weather Forecasts (ECMWF).[50]

In August 2020, Lightmatter,[51] a Boston-based start-up founded in 2017, launched their AI photonic processor; a "3D-stacked chip package" with "over a billion FinFET transistors, tens of thousands of photonic arithmetic units, and hundreds of record-setting data converters."[52] Another player in the market is Paris-based LightOn, which develops optical processing units (OPUs) that can be used in AI to boost machine learning tasks. Their photonic AI chips are built on their maiden photonic core, *Nitro*, which uses only 30 Watts of electricity to perform 3 PetaOp/s, which is 3,000,000,000,000,000 or three quadrillion operations per second.

Other notable players in the market are Fathom Computing[53] and Lightelligence.[54] Even the big-name tech giant, Nvidia, is planning to use photonics to supersede traditional electrical data transfer with optical data transfer. Nvidia plans to develop an optical NVlink alternative able to send data upward of 20 to 100 meters using only four pico Joules per bit (4 pJ/b), far superior to the conventional NVLink 2.0 chip that can only send signals to 0.3 meters while using double the power (8 pJ/b).[55]

While many tech firms in the photonic space have started off with photonic–electronic hybrids, continuing breakthroughs in optical infrastructure will slowly yield the hardware that will steadily materialize the prospects of pure optical computing systems.

---

[50] https://optalysys.com/projects-gallery

[51] https://lightmatter.co/

[52] "Lightmatter Introduces Optical Processor to Speed Compute for Next-Generation Artificial Intelligence." *insideBIGDATA*, https://insidebigdata.com/2020/08/20/lightmatter-introduces-optical-processor-to-speed-compute-for-next-generation-artificial-intelligence/ (accessed August 20, 2020).

[53] www.fathomcomputing.com/

[54] www.lightelligence.ai/

[55] Aleksandar, K. 2020. "NVIDIA is Preparing Co-Packaged Photonics for NVLink." *TechPowerUp.com*, www.techpowerup.com/276139/nvidia-is-preparing-co-packaged-photonics-for-nvlink (accessed December 18, 2020).

Biological Computing

The speedy stride of modern innovation is crystalizing several alternative computing technologies, some of which are so unusual that they seem the stuff of science fiction. But the fact of the matter is that any system that can receive specific inputs, transform those inputs, and exude specific reciprocal outputs can hypothetically be harnessed for computation and/or data storage. This makes computation and data storage possible in the most unconventional of systems.

Scientists and researchers are even looking at biological systems as plausible platforms for processing and/or storing data. Traditional computation requires the input–transform–output process. Bio nanoscience researchers hope to use proteins, genes, and other biological components to create biological circuits that can receive input, transform it according to certain rules or logic algorithms, and produce consequent results.[56] This is actually very clever because biological organisms by nature are essentially biological computers based on codes embedded in DNA and which are expressed through proteins to create the larger organism.

Researchers are exploring DNA, proteins, and other organic molecules or metabolic pathways to process, store, and retrieve data, thereby creating functioning biocomputers. Biocomputers may compute through logic operations in a variety of ways: by harnessing chemical reactions within biological media (biochemical computers); utilizing the physicality of three-dimensional configurations of molecules (biomechanical computers); capitalizing on the electrical conductivities of biological media or systems; or finally, using the movement of motor proteins or bacteria through microscopic networks (network or network-based biocomputing).

DNA Computing

DNA computing is an obvious application for biocomputing, which holds incredible promise because of the proven capacity of DNA to hold tons of

---

[56] Grozinger, L., M. Amos, T.E. Gorochowski, P. Carbonell, D.A. Oyarzún, R. Stoof, . . . and A. Goñi-Moreno. 2019. "Pathways to Cellular Supremacy in Biocomputing." *Nat Commun* 10, no. 5250. https://doi.org/10.1038/s41467-019-13232-z

complex genetic information coding for entire organisms. A proof of concept of DNA computing was demonstrated in 1994 by a researcher at the University of Southern California, Leonard Adlerman, who used DNA as a computational system to solve a seven-node Hamiltonian Graph (or traceable path) problem. Contemporary DNA computing research efforts are targeting such tangible outcomes as DNA logic gates,[57] DNA chips or integrated circuits,[58] and DNA artificial neural networks.[59]

Neurocomputing and Wetware

Neurocomputing is a field concerned with creating artificial organic brains or organic components (wetware) that can be utilized for biological computation, data transmission, or information storage. One proof of concept was performed in 1999 by William Ditto. Ditto and a crew of scientists from Emory University and Georgia Institute of Technology used leech neurons to develop a simple wetware computer that could perform rudimentary addition.[60]

Potential Applications

The concept of being able to perform calculations with biological systems is proven but the tech is still in its infancy and has not reached a level of commercial feasibility. The potential of the technology, however, is enormous.

---

[57] Song, T., A. Eshra, S. Shah, H. Bui, D. Fu, M. Yang, . . . and J. Reif. 2019. "Fast and Compact DNA Logic Circuits Based on Single-Stranded Gates Using Strand-Displacing Polymerase." *Nature Nanotechnology* 14, 1075–1081. https://doi.org/10.1038/s41565-019-0544-5

[58] Gerasimova, Y.V., and D.M. Kolpashchikov. 2016. "Angew." *Chemical Communications* 55, 10244. https://doi.org/10.1002/anie.201603265

[59] Greene, T. 2018. "Scientists Created An Artificial Neural Network Out Of DNA." *TNW*, https://thenextweb.com/artificial-intelligence/2018/07/05/scientists-created-an-artificial-neural-network-out-of-dna/ (accessed July 5, 2018).

[60] Chase, V.D. 1999. "Team Develops Biological Computer." *Nat Med* 5, 722. https://doi.org/10.1038/10437

Organic platforms for data storage could prove to be insusceptible to typical threats to traditional storage systems, like electromagnetic pulses (EMP). DNA computing has limitless possibilities. DNA is an incredibly resilient repository of genetic information even after the death of living tissue, so much so that we have been able to access the genomes of ancient humans from as far back as 430,000 years ago[61] and the DNA of ancient rhinos from 1.7 million years ago.[62]

One obvious use (or perhaps, misuse) of DNA computing and data storage would be in the intelligence community for clandestine operations. Important information could be stored in biological substrates or embedded in the living tissues or DNA of living subjects for covert transportation. But this also has the danger of being adopted by dubious parties and criminal elements for more malevolent purposes.

Overall, the progress of DNA nanoscience will invariably lead to continuing advances in our ability to reshape DNA for our purposes, correct genetic defects, and possibly end many diseases for good.

How Do We Prepare?

The future impact of biological computing on the business landscape is hard to project as we are presently only stealing glimpses of what future biocomputing products and solutions may look like. But it is still important, especially for tech professionals, to be aware that the concept exists, has been proven, and is being steadily developed.

From a career development perspective, enthusiastic business/tech professionals wanting to gain certified competency to prepare for the arrival of the biocomputing may not have to worry. In my view, it is possible that commercial users of biocomputing will not need further

---

[61] Specktor, B. 2020. "World's Oldest Human DNA Found in 800,000-Year-Old Tooth of a Cannibal." *Live Science*, www.livescience.com/oldest-human-ancestor-dna-homo-antecessor.html (accessed April 3, 2020).

[62] Daley, J. 2019. "1.7-Million-Year-Old Rhino Tooth Provides Oldest Genetic Information Ever Studied." *Smithsonian Magazine*, www.smithsonianmag.com/smart-news/million-year-old-rhino-tooth-provides-oldest-dna-data-180973117/ (accessed September 12, 2019).

certifications beyond the IT skills and programming languages required for conventional computing applications. But perhaps, because bio systems can also code beyond the two factors of zero and one, zealous professionals could brush up on quantum or nonbinary computing languages. But that is as far as a business professional may need to go to embrace biocomputing in their career, unless one is into tech development, in which case a few distance learning courses in basic cell biology and genetics will give an elementary understanding of the concepts behind biological nanoscience.

Artificial Intelligence (AI)

The Digital Revolution fostered great strides in the quest for AI; nonetheless, computers are still not truly intelligent. They can be calibrated to analyze information or return specific outputs but ultimately, they must be programmed in the first instance. The push for more proactive computing power has spurred research efforts into IT systems that can learn, or more aptly, machines that can program themselves in response to a variety of sensory or experiential data, much like humans.

A human is born into the world, blank, with no knowledge of language or the ways of society, but rather possesses just a few primal instincts to eat, sleep, and so on, as well as some preprogrammed involuntary actions such as heartbeat, digestion, and respiration. Over time, the brain analyzes data from sensory inputs such as sound and sight, and begins to pick out patterns to gain an understanding of language, identity, gender, and the world. This is what computer scientists seek to do with computers.

This section of the chapter is an overview of the field of AI, the state of the science, its relevance to business, and how we can prepare for the rise of true AI.

Types of AI

In tech terms, AI is broadly defined as the ability of machines to mimic the reasoning, mental processes, or actions of humans or higher animals. AI can be classified into two broad groups according to the level of intelligence simulated.

Weak AI, Artificial Narrow Intelligence (ANI) or *Narrow AI*, refers to a system programmed to perform a singular or narrow set of functions, often with a view to automating convoluted, repetitive, or protracted tasks. Examples include virtual personal assistants and website assistants that convey permutations, variations, and combinations of preprogrammed or supervised responses to precise queries. These include Alexa (Amazon), Siri (Apple), Google Assistant, and the computer modes of video games. Weak AI may simulate human cognition but in actuality, works via supervised programming; therefore, it lacks general intelligence and can rather be said to have *specific* intelligence. Weak AI is useful in analyzing big data and therefore finds application in sorting news feeds, suggesting online purchases, sorting e-mails, or flagging spam.[63]

Strong AI or *Artificial General Intelligence (AGI)* refers to any theoretical or real system designed with cognitive abilities or general intelligence, and that can therefore process data by clustering and association. Such *true AI* systems can learn unsupervised or program themselves to varying degrees without human intervention and will hence exhibit varied outputs for identical inputs, based on their varied resumes or portfolios of experiential data. The unsupervised programming capability of strong AI makes it applicable to a broader range of purposes than narrow AI.

So, while narrow AI only *simulates* human cognition, strong AI transcends this to emulate or *have* cognition and abilities such as reason, problem solving, judgment, planning, learning, communication, sentience, and sapience. Strong AI does not currently exist in entirety, but AI systems have been built that feature aspects of unsupervised programming and cognitive learning abilities.[64,65]

---

[63] Frankenfield, J. 2021. "Weak AI." *Investopedia*, www.investopedia.com/terms/w/weak-ai.asp (accessed February 25, 2021).

[64] IBM Cloud Education. 2020. "Strong AI." *IBM*, www.ibm.com/cloud/learn/strong-ai (accessed August 31, 2020).

[65] Frankenfield, J. 2020. "Strong AI." *Investopedia*, www.investopedia.com/terms/s/strong-ai.asp (accessed August 28, 2020).

The field that governs the programming of artificial systems to imitate human intelligence is referred to as *knowledge engineering*.[66] It has several general subfields.

Machine Learning

Machine learning is considered a subfield of AI and is concerned with a computer or AI system being able to learn from new data sets on its own, unsupervised or without human intervention, via the use of algorithms that enable it to identify data, tease out patterns, and make projections. Such systems should be able to handle big data and continually adjust to new information. Naturally, they may be of immense value in financial sectors for optimization of portfolios, trend analysis, and fraud detection.

Deep learning, deep structured learning, or *deep neural learning* is an aspect of machine learning that is concerned with designing AI learning systems to mimic human cognition and be able to analyze raw, unstructured, and unlabeled data; to deduce patterns; and to make decisions, all unsupervised. Deep learning pertains to the quest to develop *artificial neural networks (ANNs)*: synthetic learning pathways that aim to model and imitate the biological neural networks of human brains.

ANNs are characterized by webs of interconnected neurons or nodes, which process input signals through different layers and at variable levels using an internal weighting system, and which then verify the precision of outputs using a set of learning protocols called backward propagation of error, or simply backpropagation. Deep learning systems process data in a hierarchical, nonlinear fashion, unlike other more classical machine learning systems that operate linearly.

Uses of AI

The conceivable uses of AI are endless and span all industries and functions humans currently occupy. This is because true AI may be able to detect objects, think, make decisions, and speak naturally.

---

[66] Frankenfield, J. 2021. "Knowledge Engineering." *Investopedia*, www.investopedia.com/terms/k/knowledge-engineering.asp (accessed March 9, 2021).

One of the uses of AI is *Natural Language Processing* (NLP), which refers to the application of AI to deciphering and understanding languages. The general goals of NLP are the advancement of computers to a level that they can be communicated with through natural speech rather than through typographical input; and secondly, machine translation, for the universal usability of computers across borders. NLP has the potential to eliminate borders by creating a more seamless digital world with smooth transitions in digital experience regardless of one's geographical location or the person being communicated to. Using NLP one can send an e-mail in a language and the recipient can receive it in another.

A similar application of AI is in *machine translation* (MT). Here, AI goes beyond basic word-for-word translations and instead, tries to use a deeper cognitive understanding of languages, figures of speech, and dual meanings to create more accurate native-fluency translations of languages.

Other potential applications of AI are for improved data security, enhanced robotics and automation, and more intelligent chatbots and websites.

Threats to Human Workforces

Some feel that a full spectrum of AI capabilities could threaten all classes of jobs, with weak AI threatening low- to medium-skilled jobs, while AGI or strong AI, being cognitive, will threaten highly skilled or creative jobs. However, many researchers express skepticism at such a bleak outlook and reckon that, like in the industrial revolutions, AI will merely cause a shift in the nature of workforces.[67] As low-level tasks become automated or replaced by AI, job descriptions may start to skew toward supervisory or managerial functions.

AI Courses and Certifications

Considering that AI is already a heavy buzzword—even though the full arrival of the technology is still imminent—and foreseeing the massive impact it is likely to have on the business landscape, many business

---

[67] Frankenfield, J. n.d. "Strong AI." Investopedia.

professionals may think it prudent to gain some certified competencies in the technology, whether to keep their CVs competitive or to enhance their understanding of the AI playing field. The good news is that a range of relatively short, inexpensive online courses are available from credible, name-brand institutions that are recognized by managers and HR teams around the world.

For those looking to invest in a solid, industry-standard certification, the Artificial Intelligence Board of America (ARTiBA) offers the *Artificial Intelligence Engineer* (*AIE*)[68] credential. The AIE has the twofold advantage of being globally available and globally accepted as a recognized certification of knowledge in enterprise-level AI. The certification examination at the end of the course is taken online at home or office after a prescreening process that approves the computer and the venue. The course comes in three tracks, each tied to the entry qualifications of candidates: associate degree (AIE™ Track 1), bachelor's degree (AIE Track 2), and master's degree (AIE Track 3). The AIE is comprehensive and covers each function of AI, including Machine Learning, Supervised and Unsupervised Learning, Deep Learning, Reinforced Learning, Cognitive Computing, and Natural Language Processing.

MIT is offering a six-week online course, *Artificial Intelligence: Implications for Business Strategy*,[69] which is structured in flexible modules, requiring about six to eight hours a week of online work. The course, which focuses on AI technology as it relates to business, is run by both the MIT Sloan School of Management and the MIT Computer Science and Artificial Intelligence Laboratory. A certificate is issued after the course.

IBM has two certifications available on Coursera, namely the *IBM Applied AI Professional Certificate*[70] and the *IBM AI Engineering Professional Certificate*,[71] suitable for newbies and developers, respectively. IBM

---

[68] www.artiba.org/certification/artificial-intelligence-certification

[69] https://executive-education-online.mit.edu/presentations/lp/mit-artificial-intelligence-online-short-course/

[70] www.coursera.org/professional-certificates/applied-artifical-intelligence-ibm-watson-ai

[71] www.coursera.org/professional-certificates/ai-engineer

also has other AI courses[72] on the edX platform, which are self-paced and offer certificates upon completion.

For curious novices and enthusiasts interested in deepening their knowledge of machine learning without a certificate, *Google AI*[73] offers a ton of free, state-of-the-art educational tools and resources including APIs, open-source projects, and datasets.

---

[72] www.edx.org/learn/artificial-intelligence
[73] https://ai.google/education/

CHAPTER 5

Connectivity, IoT, and a Smarter World

Having discussed—in the previous chapter—promising technologies in computing power and AI, let us now move on to developments related to connectivity.

5G

5G is the latest of five technology generations of broadband cellular networks and is about a hundred times stronger than its predecessor, 4G.[1] Although research into 5G started as far back as 2008 in South Korea,[2] it took almost a decade of product development in various countries before the global commercial rollout of 5G began in 2019.[3,4]

Cellular networks slice up service areas into smaller zones called cells, which are covered through a network of transceivers and antennae mounted on a variety of cell towers.[5] Cellular technology runs on invisible

---

[1] Duffy, C. 2020. "The Big Differences Between 4G And 5G." *CNN Business*, https://edition.cnn.com/2020/01/17/tech/5g-technical-explainer/index.html (accessed January 17, 2020).

[2] Williams, H. 2020. "A Timeline Of 5G Development: From 1979 To Now." www.techadvisor.co.uk/feature/small-business/timeline-of-5g-development-3788816/ (accessed April 22, 2020).

[3] Kenneth, L., and J.M. Park. 2019. "Who Was First to Launch 5G? Depends Who You Ask." *Reuters*, www.reuters.com/article/us-telecoms-5g/who-was-first-to-launch-5g-depends-who-you-ask-idUSKCN1RH1V1 (accessed April 5, 2019).

[4] "When was 5G Introduced?" *News Center*, Verizon, www.verizon.com/about/our-company/5g/when-was-5g-introduced (accessed December 6, 2019).

[5] "What Is a Cell Tower and How Does a Cell Tower Work?" *Millman National Land Services*, https://millmanland.com/company-news/what-is-a-cell-tower-and-how-does-a-cell-tower-work/ (accessed April 26, 2021).

radio waves that are in a lower frequency band—about 3 kHz to 300 GHz—of the electromagnetic wave spectrum below microwaves, infrared and visible light, and which travel at the speed of light. Radio waves range in wavelength from about 100 kilometers for the lowest frequencies to around 1 millimeter for the highest frequencies.[6]

Successive generations of cellular networks have progressively moved toward higher frequencies and greater bandwidths to achieve higher speeds and improve signal quality. Normally, lower frequency radio waves carry less energy but have longer ranges and better penetration through obstacles. Conversely, radio waves higher up the electromagnetic spectrum carry more energy and may offer higher bandwidth, transmission quality, and network speeds, but have lower coverage or penetration through obstacles because of significant signal attenuation (reduction in signal strength). Network providers must navigate this paradox to provide a seamless compromise between speed and coverage.

The first generation of wireless or mobile cellular telecommunications, 1G, which arose in late 1979[7] and reigned during the 1980s was built on analog radio signal infrastructure, had transmission speeds of up to about 2.4 Kbps (kilobits per second), and could only handle voice calls. Cellular networks then moved to digital with the arrival of 2G, which had higher bandwidth and therefore could handle text messaging via 160-character Short Message Service (SMS), 1,600-character Multimedia Messaging Service (MMS), or connection to the Internet. Speeds were up to 50 kbps with General Packet Radio Service (GPRS) or 1 Mbps (megabits per second) with Enhanced Data Rates for GSM Evolution (EDGE).

3G, which had higher frequencies in the 1.5 to 2.8 GHz range, came on the scene in 1998 with higher bandwidths reaching 20 MHz and speeds of up to 2 Mbps on static devices or 384 Kbps on moving devices

---

[6] "What are Radio Waves?" *NASA*, www.nasa.gov/directorates/heo/scan/communications/outreach/funfacts/txt_radio_spectrum.html (accessed April 1, 2021).

[7] Chan. A.S. 2018. "A Brief History of 1G Mobile Communication Technology." *Xoxzo*, https://blog.xoxzo.com/en/2018/07/24/history-of-1g/ (accessed July 24, 2018).

in cars, trains, and the like.[8] This significant improvement in bandwidth heralded the age of mobile Internet and video calling.

Deployed the late 2000s, 4G bumped us up into the true age of fast Internet. 4G had higher frequencies in the 20-MHz bandwidth sector with a peak capacity of 400 Mbps and speeds 50 to 500 times faster than 3G. Observable speeds can be lower when too many users share available sector capacity. With speeds up to tens or hundreds of Mbps on static devices or tens of Mbps on moving devices in cars, trains, or on foot, 4G fostered a new wave of applications and rich multiplayer multimedia experiences, and was able to handle video conferencing and high-definition (HD) mobile TV.

5G builds upon the success story of 4G with a further increase in frequency range. Unlike previous generations, 5G is comprised of three bands configured to give decent- to high-speed Internet over a wide range of conditions such as location, motion, and urban obstacles.

Low-band spectrum 5G is usually between the 600 and 850 MHz bands and is thus sometimes called sub-1 GHz spectrum 5G. The advantage of this band is that range is higher, thus transmission can be carried over a greater coverage area with decent penetration through obstacles and walls. This band is also used by current 4G LTE (Long-Term Evolution), but 5G's fifth-generation transmission technologies boost to higher speeds than fourth-generation LTE. The high saturation of customers operating at these frequencies means these low bands are nearing depletion in most wired countries; sometimes peak data speeds only go up to about 100 Mbps.[9]

Mid-band spectrum 5G is located in the 2.5 GHz range of spectrum and offers faster speeds than low-band, with peak speeds up to 1 Gbps. On the downside, it has a decreased range and lower penetration through obstacles and buildings than low-band spectrum 5G. To counter this, networks compensate by using unique technologies called Massive MIMO

---

[8] "What Is the Difference Between 3G, 4G and 5G?" *News Center*, Verizon, www.verizon.com/about/our-company/5g/difference-between-3g-4g-5g (accessed November 18, 2019).

[9] de Looper, C. 2021. "What Is 5G? Everything You Need to Know." *Digital Trends*, www.digitaltrends.com/mobile/what-is-5g/ (accessed March 15, 2021).

(multiple-input multiple-output) and Beamforming to better manage penetration and coverage. Massive MIMO is a multiple-user MIMO, which groups large arrays of antennas onto a base station to create multiple beams to serve many terminals at the same time.[10] Beamforming, instead of transmitting signals in all directions, creates a faster, reliable connection to a receiving device by focusing wireless signals directly toward it, like a beam.

High-band spectrum or ultrafast 5G is higher up the spectrum at 30 GHz and is sometimes called millimeter wave or mmWave because it uses exceedingly small 1- to 10-millimeter waves. These high-frequency waves offer blistering speeds, with peak speed of up to 10 Gbps, and very low latency (delay between signal origination and signal reception), but are so small that their penetration is bad. Because of this rapid attenuation, coverage or range can be low. So, though high-band spectrum 5G offers highest performance, networks have to counter its low coverage area and low building penetration by having erecting high densities of smaller cells, especially in built-up urban areas and cities. Here too, Massive MIMO and Beamforming technologies can boost performance.

Using a seamless transition of these three 5G bands, networks can offer fast 5G service to users, whether stationary or moving, indoors or out in the open, though bandwidths will continuously vary. Despite the higher frequencies and bandwidths, a lot of the improvements of 5G over 4G actually come from enhancements in transmission technology, like MIMO.

Drivers Behind the Technology

A key driving force behind the ongoing innovation of cellular network technology is the continual adoption and proliferation of mobile, online applications, and the Internet of Things (IoT) to the point that even household devices and all manner of appliances are going online. In the near future, one person could in effect have over 10, 20, or any large number of personal devices or IoT sensors connected to or transmitting

---

[10] "What is Massive MIMO." *Wireless Future*, https://ma-mimo.ellintech.se/what-is-massive-mimo/ (accessed April 26, 2021).

over the Internet. This represents a big swell in demand for connectivity and bandwidth. In fact, Cisco's Annual Internet Report (2018–2023) projects that networked devices, which numbered 18.4 billion globally in 2018, will grow to 29.3 billion by 2023.[11]

Controversies

Each new generation of cellular network has triggered concerns about public health, particularly over fears of cancer and heating effects on the brain or cell structures. 5G, being run on relatively higher radio frequencies is no exception.

There are many enduring misgivings about 5G, some understandable and others, wild and outlandish. Some temperate debates center on calls for research into whether the higher radiofrequencies of 5G may adversely affect the immune system and make people increasingly susceptible to diseases, cancers, and infections.[12] More extreme controversies claim that exposure to the radiofrequency fields of 5G could be partly to blame for the ferociousness of the Covid-19 pandemic, complimented by purported bird deaths around 5G towers.[13]

The jury is still out on some of these disputes, but there is currently no proof of ill effects on the immune system from exposure to radio frequency fields. Scientifically, cellular radiation is not considered harmful.[14] This is because the radio waves used in cellular technologies are

---

[11] "Cisco Annual Internet Report (2018–2023) White Paper." *CISCO*, www.cisco.com/c/en/us/solutions/collateral/executive-perspectives/annual-internet-report/white-paper-c11-741490.pdf (accessed March 9, 2020).

[12] Hewings-Martin, Y. 2019. "Is 5G Technology Bad for our Health?" *Medical News Today*, www.medicalnewstoday.com/articles/326141 (accessed August 23, 2019).

[13] Ahmed, W., J. Downing, M. Tuters, and P. Knight. 2020. "Four Experts Investigate How the 5G Coronavirus Conspiracy Theory Began." *The Conversation*, https://theconversation.com/four-experts-investigate-how-the-5g-coronavirus-conspiracy-theory-began-139137 (accessed June 11, 2020).

[14] "Do Cell Phones Pose a Health Hazard?" *US Food and Drug Administration*, www.fda.gov/radiation-emitting-products/cell-phones/do-cell-phones-pose-health-hazard (accessed February 10, 2020).

not ionizing. Ionizing radiation has high energy content and can detach electrons from atoms, ionizing them; therefore, exposure can cause chemical bonds in the body to break or get damaged, sometimes resulting in uncontrolled cell growth and the emergence of cancer. This is apparently not possible with the nonionizing radiation used in cellular technology because the energy content is not as much. So far, thermal heating is the only proven effect of exposure to the radiofrequency radiation of cellular networks. In fact, to cause chemical breakage in human tissues, we would have to go up the electromagnetic spectrum to higher ultraviolet radiation, X-rays, and gamma rays.

The Rise of 6G

6G is the next generation of cellular networks and will almost certainly rely on submillimeter waves. Big tech companies are already working to fashion solutions to meet the projected connectivity demands of society for the next decade.

Though it was launched in 2020, 5G had been worked on as far back as 2013 by Samsung. Similarly, 6G is scheduled to roll out around 2028 or 2030 but it is already being implemented on a testing basis. Prototype 6G chips have already been built. 6G will enable a hyper-connected society where the main users of cellular will be both humans and machines.

6G could have a tenth of the latency of 5G and be fifty times faster,[15] a hundred times more reliable, and handle ten times more devices.[16] One would theoretically be able to download over a hundred hours of Netflix in a second. But why do we need such blistering speeds? Because by 2030, data-hungry emerging technologies may have become fully mainstream, requiring unprecedented levels of instantaneous connectivity.

---

[15] Indip, I. 2021. "6G is coming to make good on the promises of 5G." Interview by Olga Putsykina, *Fraunhofer Institute for Reliability and Microintegration IZM*, www.izm.fraunhofer.de/en/news_events/tech_news/6g-is-coming-to-make-good-on-the-promises-of-5G.html (accessed August 21, 2021).

[16] Mohamed, M. 2021. "From 5G to 6G: What could it look like?" *Light Reading*, https://www.lightreading.com/6g/from-5g-to-6g-what-could-it-look-like/a/d-id/767711 (accessed August 21, 2021).

These include quantum computing, augmented reality, and IoT devices. Autonomous vehicles, in particular, may have low margins of tolerance for drops in connectivity as they will depend on real-time navigation while in motion to keep people safe.

There are, nevertheless, some challenges to a 6G-enabled future. Even current 5G millimeter waves are easily blocked by obstacles such as trees and urban obstacles. 6G may have to overcome the higher attenuation of its submillimeter waves by embedding antenna technology into domestic infrastructure like furniture for a fee or incentive—thereby democratizing cellular transmission—or by incorporating tech into 6G devices that make them act as both receivers and transmitters.[17]

Internet of Things (IoT)

IoT is the incorporation of sensors and/or connected technology into all manner of objects, enabling them to collect data and/or to connect to each other or other systems through the Internet, or in some cases, intranets.

The term "Internet of Things" was fashioned in 1999 by Kevin Ashton in reference to the potential of radiofrequency identification (RFID) technologies to make possible an Internet characterized by more online traffic from things than online traffic from actual people. Some have postulated that this is already a reality and that online traffic from things surpassed human online traffic between 2003 and 2010, during which time the ratio of thing- versus people-generated traffic grew from 0.08 to 1.84.[18]

The Rise of IoT

The rise of IoT was enabled principally by the miniaturization of MOS transistors, allowing tiny sensors to be embedded into almost anything to

---

[17] Mrwhosetheboss. 2020. "6G - Explained!" YouTube video, www.youtube.com/watch?v=AvcAovqG5Kk (accessed September 25, 2020).

[18] Evans, D. 2011. "The Internet of Things: How the Next Evolution of the Internet Is Changing Everything." CISCO White Paper, www.cisco.com/c/dam/en_us/about/ac79/docs/innov/IoT_IBSG_0411FINAL.pdf

collect and transmit a wide variety of data. This miniaturization of sensor technology has given rise to an era of *smart* devices. A smart device or object is one that can record or transmit data about one or more properties and/or communicate with other devices or platforms through the Internet or through intranets.

Other enabling factors of IoT include the predominance of the Internet and advancements in remote digital communication technologies such as RFID, near-field communication (NFC), 3G to 5G cellular networks, and wireless fidelity (Wi-Fi) broadband technologies.

Applications of IoT and Smart Technologies

The proliferation of smart devices is creating a future where an amazing array of personal assets and data may be monitored online. The fantasy lifestyles of science fiction are now a reality. Through smart technologies, it is now possible to autonomously manage devices in our homes, offices, and even in/on our bodies.

Smart technologies are moving medical measurements out of the domain of traditional health care facilities and placing those capabilities into the realm of individuals in the form of smart watches, wearables, and other devices that can check and track heart rate, temperature, blood pressure, respiratory rate, and sugar level on the fly or in real time. This convenient capturing of continuous health data empowers individuals to better manage their well-being and allows the early identification of risk factors or warning signs of medical crises before they occur.

Smart shoes, watches, and other wearables encourage an active lifestyle by counting our daily steps, tracking sleep, and monitoring movement. Some apps even gamify exercise by allowing peer-to-peer challenges via these smart wearables.

The application of smart technologies to home appliances and tasks in the domestic sphere has created integrated solutions for automated or *smart* homes. Robot vacuum cleaners like the Neato Botvac D7 and iRobot Roomba i7+ continuously scan and clean floors, while some smart fridges can automatically detect stock levels and reorder specific groceries. Digital assistants can manage access protocols for each household member and customize lighting, play music, and brew coffee to their preference. Digital assistants can also manage power, heating, and other utilities to reduce wastage and streamline consumption.

Many variants of smart homes are commercially available in several markets with varied price ranges and many options. Depending on whether they are built as integrated solutions or customized singly, smart homes offer—to varying degrees—a release from laborious and repetitive chores; cost savings from leaner, on-demand stocking of groceries and consumables; and optimal use of energy. Some trendy smart home systems are Wink Hub, Amazon Alexa, Google Assistant, and Samsung SmartThings Hub.[19]

IoT devices and smart technologies are also finding application in industrial and commercial spheres. From transportation to construction and manufacturing, smart tech is increasing managerial visibility, creating convenience, eliminating wastage, reducing costs, and increasing safety. In agriculture, IoT is revolutionizing farm management by helping to better monitor the conditions of crops and livestock or to streamline irrigation, feeding, and health care.

Smart tech and IoT are also making inroads into urban planning and infrastructural sectors, and helping public regulatory agencies with enhanced energy management, environmental monitoring, security surveillance, and traffic management. With the gradual deployment of smart devices and IoT into every sphere of society, we are heading into an era of smart homes, smart streets, smart buildings, smart communities, and ultimately, smart cities.

Smart Cities

A smart city is one that utilizes data analytics and AI to analyze big data from smart tech or IoT devices deployed in domestic, commercial, and public spheres to optimize city management for the good of its citizens and the planet.

---

[19] Forsey, C. 2021. "The 13 Best Smart Home Devices & Systems of 2021." *HubSpot*, https://blog.hubspot.com/marketing/smart-home-devices (accessed February 24, 2021).

High-speed computing, AI, IoT, and ICT are the main enablers of smart cities. Smart cities harness intelligent networks of IoT devices connected through wireless technologies and are an amalgamation of progressively smaller units of smart vehicles, smart homes, smart lighting, smart appliances, smart utilities, and more, each optimized for utility and energy efficiency.

Citizens can sign up to and enjoy the optimized benefits of smart cities by connecting to a city's smart services through personal devices and phones or through smart interfaces in smart homes, offices, or public spaces.

Principal drivers behind smart cities include convenience and the optimization of traffic and resource flows. All manner of benefits can be derived from the implementation of smart systems in cities. Traffic congestion is minimized by traffic lights or stoplights that sense varying traffic flows and optimize timings of traffic signals to prioritize congested roads in real time. Trash collection can be automated via smart garbage cans for when trash cans are full as opposed to having fixed schedules for collection, which may be unnecessary, too early, or too late. Smart identity solutions can enable the use of digital credentials to verify ID, driver's licenses, and permits through integrated devices like smartphones, and thereby offer simpler and speedier access to public services such as parking, police, emergency services, transport, and entertainment.

Important sectors tackled by smart systems to make a city smart include security, health care, mobility, water, waste management, energy, and housing. Famous hubs with smart city initiatives include Dubai, Singapore, Boston, Oslo, Copenhagen, and Amsterdam.[20]

The rise of IoT, smart tech, and smart communities has serious implications for business. Smart companies thrive better energy-wise and smart cities offer novel business avenues and job opportunities. All over the world, brave businesses have proactively taken the lead in embracing smart concepts so as to be firmly established and ahead of the curve when these technologies become mainstream.

[20] Kosowatz, J. 2020. "Top 10 Growing Smart Cities." *ASME*, https://asme.org/topics-resources/content/top-10-growing-smart-cities (accessed February 3, 2020).

Yet, there are still some serious concerns about the pervasiveness of IoT, especially in the areas of privacy and security. Some factions fear that the ubiquitous nature of smart tech may be compromised by malicious agents for criminal activities, or by governments for intrusive and unwarranted surveillance. Consequently, governments and tech companies are having to address these concerns, while they collaborate to shape the development of international standards to regulate the IoT space.

CHAPTER 6

Virtual Worlds

Previously discussed advances in computing power, data storage, and connectivity are all geared toward the same end: better digital lifestyles. But what about *how* we experience the digital world? This chapter will delve into some applications, devices, and interfaces that are driving seamless interactions with the digital space and steadily creating an age where the real world and virtual world merge.

Virtual Reality (VR)

The advent of electronic virtual environments was sparked chiefly by the digital revolution. Digital video games, in particular, drew VR to the fore as millions delved into a range of alternative electronic realities, from simple ones like the brick game, Tetris, to more sophisticated ones like Prince of Persia and Doom, which featured working simulations of gravity and other physical laws. The development of professional simulators for training pilots, astronauts, and submariners further pushed the boundaries of computer science as physical laws needed to be replicated as close to reality as possible. With the arrival of the Internet, VR burgeoned and gamers could compete with friends or strangers across the globe, instantaneously.

Decades of successive improvements in graphics hardware, software, computer processors, and other technologies have empowered developers to consistently create new virtual environments or simulations that are unparalleled in their realism. Currently, spurred on by new leaps in emerging technologies such as blockchain and AI, virtual worlds are emerging that offer alternative virtual lifestyles replete with unprecedented levels of interaction and that also come complete with their own virtual economies and commerce.

The commercial activities within these virtual economies are gradually gaining prominence. These worlds constitute radical new channels for business development, lead generation, marketing, and sales. It is thus important for business professionals and entrepreneurs to be aware of their existence and potential.

Virtual Worlds

Though their distinction can sometimes be unclear, there seem to be two broad categories of VR: virtual worlds and virtual reality games (or game worlds). Virtual worlds and game worlds are digital, simulated environments that are commonly experienced through avatars and are interacted with via VR technologies like VR headsets or via regular computers and other devices.

Teenagers typically immerse themselves in game worlds such as The Sims franchise, Farmville, World of Warcraft, and Minecraft, but they are certainly not the only customers. Adults are a big customer segment for these game worlds. Virtual worlds, however, are more tailored toward adults and some of them exclude children completely. They tend to be less about gaming and more about social interaction, events, experiences, and the sale of virtual products and services.

- Second Life is the number-one virtual world across the globe with over 11 million users. At its peak, it once hosted over one million *active* residents.[1] It is not 3D and is not designed exclusively for VR headsets though it is still compatible with them; thus, most users use regular screens. With a vibrant economy, the Second Life universe is full of avenues for creative expression and fosters the establishment of professional and personal relationships. This virtual world was released in 2003 and is developed by its users, who are able to earn income, some quite substantially. Famous examples include Ailin Graef, also known by her avatar Anshe Chung, who has made millions through real estate development in Second Life.

---

[1] "Top Ten Virtual Worlds for Adults." *Stream Scheme*, www.streamscheme.com/top-ten-virtual-worlds-for-adults/ (accessed February 8, 2021).

- IMVU is another virtual world focused on social networking and which came on the scene in 2004. It has an active economy and is popular for its catalog of over 40 million virtual goods.
- Launched in 2009, Blue Mars is a popular, highly customizable virtual world. Users can use the Sandbox Editor SDK suite to create or customize the virtual world and their avatars with clothes, shops, and *massively multiplayer online games* (MMOGs or MMOs), which can host thousands of players.
- Released in 2005, Red Light Center is a virtual world that ventures into adult entertainment. It is modeled after the Red Light District of Amsterdam and has virtual entertainment venues such as bars and nightclubs, where users may spend the virtual currency called Rays and engage in adult-themed interactions.

While most virtual worlds are accessible or viewable on any screen type, there is a subgroup of 3D worlds that seem purposely built for use with VR headsets and accessories, even though they often support limited desktop modes.

- VRChat is a free social MMO virtual world that was released in 2014. Users can create intricate 3D avatars, fashion their own environments or objects, and participate in a variety of minigames or challenges with other users. When used with the right VR equipment, avatars can feature blinking, eye tracking, and audio lip syncing. This MMO is in perpetual development as users customize new worlds within it.
- Sansar[2] entered the market in 2017 and is a VR platform focused on the hosting of virtual live events, most especially concerts, which people can attend from the comfort of their home or elsewhere. Sansar facilitates a variety of interactions and actions like dancing and selfies. One can also *cop merch*

---

[2] www.sansar.com/

(acquire or buy merchandise). Users can upgrade tickets to access superpowers, VIP privileges, and special rewards, or to attend restricted meet-and-greets with their artistes. The revelry is endless as shows morph into parties and afterparties and after-afterparties. In a *new normal* of global pandemics that can force social distancing, lockdowns, and travel restrictions, platforms like Sansar provide viable options for fans to maintain their live entertainment lifestyles.

- AltspaceVR[3] is similar to and is somewhat a forerunner Sansar but also features an expansive range of other events such as meetups, classes, or even, VR church. It was launched in 2015 by the California-based start-up of the same name, which was founded in 2013 but was later acquired by Microsoft in 2017.

- Rec Room[4] is a popular VR community geared toward social interaction or games and that allows users who are not fluent in coding to create their own worlds. Apparently, there are more than a million worlds in Rec Room. Users can create 3D shapes or objects using a *marker pen* and use them to customize personal spaces called rooms, which can be published and opened to other players to visit. Players can also create additional objects or *inventions* for other users to acquire and use in their own rooms. Patronage of rooms and inventions can generate income for the players who created them. Players are paid in *tokens*, the platforms currency.

- Unlike the aforementioned VR platforms, Google Earth VR[5] is themed around the virtual exploration of an accurate simulation of the Earth, allowing people to tour the world virtually. Users can fly and walk through cities such as London and New York, or tour landmarks such as the Grand Canyon and Hoover Dam.

---

[3] https://altvr.com/
[4] https://recroom.com/
[5] arvr.google.com/earth/

Other notable mentions in the VR space include: Active Worlds,[6] Empire of Sports, Kaneva, NuVera Online, Onverse, Sony PlayStation 3 Home, Utherverse, and Meet Me.

Virtual Reality Gear

There is an amazing array of gear and accessories capable of facilitating a wide spectrum of VR experiences with varying depths of immersion. There are decent options solutions for any budget, whether low, mid-range, or high-end.

The cheapest and simplest option for a basic VR experience is Google Cardboard[7] or alternative Google-Cardboard-compatible VR headsets. These are designed to be attached to smartphones and used with VR mobile apps and games. One can purchase certified viewers or fold their own using nothing more than lenses, cardboard, rubber bands, and/or fasteners. Cardboard viewers are usually strapless and are therefore handheld.

Mid-range options for VR headsets are more sophisticated and may have additional screens, tracking sensors, and more intricate controls, all under the rough price of 150 dollars.[8] Arguably, the most well-known mid-range, phone-powered headset was the Samsung Gear VR but the company announced in May 2020 that it would discontinue support for the device and its apps. Other amazing options on the market include the LG 360 VR,[9] Zeiss VR One,[10] and Homido's Prime, V2, and Grab.[11,12]

---

[6] www.activeworlds.com/

[7] https://arvr.google.com/cardboard/

[8] Robertson, A. 2021. "The Ultimate VR Headset Buyer's Guide." *The Verge*, www.theverge.com/a/best-vr-headset-oculus-rift-samsung-gear-htc-vive-virtual-reality, (accessed April 26, 2021).

[9] www.lg.com/us/mobile-accessories/lg-LGR100AVRZTS-360-vr

[10] https://vroneus.myshopify.com/

[11] https://homido.com/en/

[12] Greenwald, W. 2021. "The Best VR Headsets for 2021." *PCMag*, www.pcmag.com/picks/the-best-vr-headsets?test_uuid=001OQhoHLBxsrrrMgWU3gQF&test_variant=b (accessed January 28, 2021).

High-end VR kits tend to be tethered, meaning they are connected to game consoles or computers that power their premium VR experiences with super graphics and motion tracking, among other things. These VR solutions can go upward of 399 dollars to beyond 700 dollars. The biggest perk of high-end headsets is positional tracking that allows you to physically move around to varying degrees, limited by the room you use and how you configure the gear. These headsets also use gamepads and/or motion controllers.

Leaders in the VR gear market include Oculus, Valve, HTC, and Sony. Oculus VR, LLC was established in Irvine, California, in 2012, but was acquired by Facebook in 2014 and moved near Facebook Headquarters in Menlo Park in the Bay Area. In 2015, Oculus worked with Samsung to produce the aforementioned, popular mid-range Gear VR. Oculus has several high-end VR solutions like the Rift models, which are tethered, and the Quest line of standalone headsets.

Valve Corporation (or Valve Software), a popular video game company based in Bellevue, Washington, released its own standalone VR headset, the *Index*, in June 2019. Valve Index's controllers can track the motion, pressure, and position of a user's hand and fingers.

HTC released its Vive VR headset in 2016 in collaboration with Valve. HTC Vive supports room scale VR, where a user can move around and interact with the virtual environment via controllers.

Sony's high-end VR headset solution is the PlayStation VR. PlayStation VR uses DualShock controller and PS Move wands.

Virtual Economies

Currently, it is estimated that virtual worlds are patronized by over 2.5 billion people who spend over $100 million a year on virtual merchandise and services.[13] The commercial prospects of these growing virtual economies are not limited to just game developers and makers of VR gear.

---

[13] Bakhtiari, K. 2020. "Welcome to Hyperreality: Where the Physical and Virtual Worlds Converge." *Forbes*, www.forbes.com/sites/kianbakhtiari/2021/12/30/welcome-to-hyperreality-where-the-physical-and-virtual-worlds-converge/?sh=236cc9b50283 (accessed December 30, 2020).

Virtual worlds provide novel channels for real-world companies to reach digital audiences to promote their brands. Some prominent, brave companies have integrated VR into their marketing strategies. For instance, Adidas, Dell, Amazon, Mercedes Benz, Intel, Cisco, Bain & Company, IBM, Microsoft, Sony, Warner Bros Music, and Wells Fargo have all had an active presence in Second Life at some point,[14] and some still do.

And then there are the other economic beneficiaries of virtual worlds; the users themselves, many of whom are able to develop real estate or digital merchandise and trade them for virtual currency, which they can cash out in real-world currency. Indeed, the value of some of these microtransactions can be quite surprising. In 2010, Club Neverdie, a popular venue in the Entropia Universe (a science-fiction MMORPG),[15] was sold for $635,000, setting a world record for the most expensive sale of a virtual object. The year before that, another piece of Entropia Universe real estate, the Crystal Space Station, sold for $333,000.[16] Virtual worlds are unleashing creativity and generating remarkable income avenues for creatives by freeing them from the burden of real-world manufacturing. More and more, artists, fashion designers, architects, and the like are able to peddle virtual products whose real-life equivalents would be expensive, implausible, or impossible to produce.

Augmented Reality (AR)

The merits of virtual reality are not exclusive to the virtual domain but are steadily being applied to enhance real world experiences. Recent years have seen growth in AR, which is simply the use of technology to superimpose digital infrastructure or virtual assets onto the real world for better informational or interactional experiences. So, while virtual reality is typically exclusive of the real world, AR (or mixed reality) is virtual reality

---

[14] Atli, D., and C. Tuncer. 2015. "Advertising in Virtual Worlds: The Example of Second Life." *Journal of Media Critiques [JMC]* 2056–9785, no. 1, 103–116. 10.17349/jmc115205

[15] www.entropiauniverse.com/

[16] "Virtual Asteroid Run as Entropia Club Sold for Profit." *BBC*, www.bbc.com/news/technology-11795098 (accessed November 19, 2010).

inclusive of reality such that one can interact instantaneously with both through a range of sensory inputs and feedback. AR is sometimes referred to as computer-mediated reality.

With the rising adoption of AR, the real world and virtual world are drawing closer together and beginning to merge in real time. Just like the case of virtual reality, gaming was a big driver in the development of AR, typified by the AR craze generated when Pokémon GO came out in 2016. The mobile game generated footfall for many businesses and with its treasure-hunt-like challenges, it facilitated active lifestyles. Yet, due to its immersive attributes and the sometimes-obscure locations of Pokémon assets, it was also known for possibly contributing to "nearly 150,000 traffic accidents, 256 deaths and economic costs of $2 billion to $7.3 billion in the first 148 days after its introduction to the US."[17]

Augmented Reality Gear

Like VR gear, AR gear come in an assortment of types at a variety of price points to fit low, mid-range, and high-end budgets. A common form of AR gear is smart glasses. These are essentially untethered spectacles that can project virtual features into one or both lenses, or which have one or more displays placed directly into the field of view.

Some AR general-purpose glasses like the Epson Moverio BT-35E and Moverio BT-40 feature high-definition (HD) displays and high-resolution cameras. One can even use the Moverio BT-35E to control a drone. The Blade Smart Glasses from Vuzix feature haptic feedback and work well with Android or iOS smartphones. Both product lines are at mid-range price points hovering somewhere between $579 and $999.[18] Another decent option used to be Focals by North—a Canadian start-up

---

[17] Revell, T. 2017. "Did Pokémon Go Really Kill 250 People in Traffic Accidents?" *NewScientist*, www.newscientist.com/article/2154881-did-pokemon-go-really-kill-250-people-in-traffic-accidents/ (accessed November 28, 2017).
[18] Dugdale, M. 2021. "Epson Moverio BT-40 and BT-40S AR Smart Glasses Available for Pre-Order." *VRWorldTech*, https://vrworldtech.com/2021/03/03/epson-moverio-bt-40-and-bt-40s-ar-smart-glasses-available-for-pre-order/ (accessed March 3, 2021).

backed by Amazon—but the company was acquired by Google in 2020, and this is generating anticipation about what wonderful new AR platforms the giant will be releasing in future. Even Apple is working on its own pair of AR smart glasses, slated for 2021 or 2022.[19]

Everysight Raptor[20] and Kopin SOLOS[21] are reasonably priced sports-themed smart glasses at about $599 and $499, respectively.[22] The Raptor is tailored for cycling and features a front camera, two microphones, an internal speaker, an integrated touchpad, and an optional controller that can be attached to a bicycle handlebar. The SOLOS is tailored to a wider variety of sports than just cycling, including running and triathlons, and has several performance trackers for speed, heart rate, power, and more. Both AR glasses can be paired with smartphones to access their respective apps.

The higher-priced ThirdEye Gen X2[23] (about $2,699)[24] is designed for professional users or students, thus users can share their point of view and receive remote assistance through live video or audio. Google Glass Enterprise Edition 2[25] and Vuzix M300[26] are also high-end options at about $999.[27,28] Both are purposed exclusively for enterprise users and are packed with powerful tools in that regard, such as powerful memory, Wi-Fi and Bluetooth connectivity, and voice control for hands-free operation.

---

[19] Kozuch, K. 2021. "Apple Glasses: Release Date, Price, Features and Leaks." *Tom's Guide*, www.tomsguide.com/news/apple-glasses (accessed April 26, 2021).

[20] https://everysight.com/product/raptor/

[21] www.kopin.com/solos/

[22] At Time of Writing (accessed April 26, 2021).

[23] https://thirdeyegen.com/x2-smart-glasses

[24] At Time of Writing, www.amazon.com/ThirdEye-X2-MR-Glasses/dp/B08GCYNCBM (accessed April 26, 2021).

[25] www.google.com/glass/tech-specs/

[26] www.vuzix.com/support/legacy-product/m300-smart-glasses

[27] At Time of Writing, www.computerworld.com/article/3519442/google-opens-up-glass-enterprise-edition-2-for-direct-purchases.html (accessed April 26, 2021).

[28] At Time of Writing, www.aniwaa.com/product/vr-ar/vuzix-m300/ (accessed April 26, 2021).

Another type of AR platform is the head-mounted display, like the Toshiba dynaEdge AR100 Viewer[29], which can fit over regular glasses to convert them into smart glasses or can be attached to headbands, lensless frames, and safety helmets. The Toshiba dynaEdge AR100 Viewer works with Toshiba's dynaEdge DE-100, which is a mobile mini-PC running Microsoft Windows. An even higher-priced but powerful option is the Microsoft HoloLens,[30] which are head-mounted display smart glasses. This amazing platform is a fully fledged computer. It can run 3D apps and is controlled by gaze, gesture, and voice (GGV) commands and can be paired with a finger-operated Clicker for scrolling and selecting.

The simplest form of AR gear is mobile AR, which is AR through smartphone apps that project AR infrastructure over live images or video captured via the mobile's camera. Other handheld solutions being developed include AR binoculars[31] and dedicated AR displays.

One of the oldest forms of AR is the heads-up display. Originally a mainstay of aviation and aerospace, heads-up displays (HUD) are now finding use in other industries, especially in cars and enterprise applications.

Fringe Interfaces and Gear

Screenless Displays

Apart from the VR and AR gear currently in vogue, scientists are exploring unconventional screenless options for accessing VR and AR (or extended reality). Screenless options can be categorized into visual image displays, retinal displays, and synaptic interfaces.

Visual image displays include previously discussed VR and AR solutions, and holographic displays. Holographic displays use a variety of technologies such as holographic film, helium neon lasers, and mirrors to display realistic 3D images or video, viewable by the naked eye without any wearables or monitors. The technology is still being developed,

---

[29] https://us.dynabook.com/smartglasses/products/index.html
[30] www.microsoft.com/en-us/hololens
[31] "Augmented Reality Binoculars." *Tech Briefs TV*, www.techbriefs.com/component/content/article/tb/tv/31292 (accessed April 26, 2021).

but holograms, when perfected, could revolutionize the telepresence and entertainment industries.

Retinal displays refer to technologies that beam images right onto the retina. Such technologies are still fledglings but hold amazing promise. Synaptic or brain–computer interfaces allow the viewing of images through direct interactions between devices and the brain. The concepts behind synaptic interfaces have already been proven and there are working examples being used in sectors such as education and communication.

Gestural Interfaces

Engineers are rapidly moving beyond touchscreen interfaces and other tactile tools to develop free-form gestural interfaces that feel effortless and natural. Such touchless, gestural ways of controlling devices are gaining attention because of their public health benefits if applied to devices in the public sphere, such as ATMs, access doors, elevators, and so on. This will be especially pertinent in a post-Covid-19 new normal.[32]

Keeping Up

Advances in VR and AR will continue to transform the tools we use in business and nonbusiness professions. They are likely to disrupt many existing tech industries and their markets. But progress is inevitable and so, therefore, is change. Business and tech professionals wishing to keep up-to-date with virtual worlds and AR should keep tabs on the gaming industry, possibly by following annual gaming conferences. Since the genesis of the technological age, gaming has played a monumental role in driving the demand for speedier connectivity, realistic graphics, radical user interfaces, and greater interaction between remote players. Thus, new tech usually makes it to gaming before it hits other sectors.

---

[32] "Chapter 1. Introducing Interactive Gestures." O'Reilly, www.oreilly.com/library/view/designing-gestural-interfaces/9780596156756/ch01.html (accessed April 26, 2021).

CHAPTER 7

Materials and Production Technologies

In this chapter, we cover a few of the latest technologies that are transforming the way we produce our artificial world. We cover some new materials and the scientific breakthroughs that allow us to engineer them.

Nanotechnology

Nanotechnology refers to the scientific discipline of engineering products or manipulating structures and processes at the nanometer level, typically one to a hundred nanometers. Being one-billionth of a meter, a nanometer is just 10 times the diameter of a hydrogen atom; nanotechnology therefore can operate at the atomic or molecular level.

To gain some perspective, consider that the width of a human hair is averagely 80,000 times the width of a nanometer. At this level, physics and chemistry behave differently from the way they behave in the micro- and macro worlds, with marked changes in the dynamics of strength, electrical conductivity, thermal conductivity, and color. The rationale for innovation at this scale is to harness these unique properties to engender increased strength, decreased weight, energy efficiency, superconductivity, and other attributes to all manner of industries such as materials science, computing, health, and so on.[1]

There are two main approaches to nanotechnology: top-down and bottom-up. The top-down approach is the use of macro- or micro processes, or remote forces like ion beams, to create products or produce effects at the nano level. This sometimes involves the etching of

---

[1] "What is Nanotechnology and What Can It Do?" *AZoNano*, www.azonano.com/article.aspx?ArticleID=1134 (accessed March 5, 2005).

material into nanoscale structures. Examples include the utilization of giant magnetoresistance (GMR) and atomic layer deposition (ALD). The bottom-up approach entails the actual manipulation of atoms or nano-level structures to engineer larger molecules or assemblages.[2] This is sometimes called "extreme nanotechnology."

There is also the function-based approach, which focuses on harnessing nanotechnology to achieve specific functionalities—such as superparamagnetism and single-molecule electronics—in products, materials, or processes. Another subfield is the biomimetic approach that harnesses biological systems for use in nanotechnology. This includes the manipulation of viruses and biomolecules.

Nanomaterials are often classified into four categories based on dimensionality: 0D (zero-dimensional), 1D (one-dimensional), 2D (two-dimensional), and 3D (three-dimensional).

The Rise of Nanotech: Current and Emerging Applications

In 1959, physicist Richard Feynman, a physicist, delivered a talk at CalTech under the theme, *There's Plenty of Room at the Bottom*. In it, he laid out the plausible dynamics of working with single atoms or molecules, concepts that would come to underpin the science of nanotechnology, even though the term had not been formulated yet. Then in 1974, Norio Taniguchi, a professor at Tokyo University of Science, fashioned the term *nano-technology* to outline semiconductor processes at the nanometer level.[3] Finally, in 1981, mankind was finally able to actually view single atoms through the invention of the scanning tunneling microscope. The age of nanotechnology had dawned.

However, K. Eric Drexler is largely credited with popularizing the term through his 1986 book, *Engines of Creation: The Coming Era of*

---

[2] "Manufacturing at the Nanoscale." *Nano.gov*, www.nano.gov/nanotech-101/what/manufacturing (accessed April 27, 2021).
[3] "What Is Nanotechnology and Why Is It Important?" *Nanowerk*, www.nanowerk.com/nanotechnology/introduction/introduction_to_nanotechnology_1.php (accessed April 28, 2021).

Nanotechnology.[4] This work discussed, among other things, the concept of nano devices, called assemblers, capable of self-replicating or manufacturing objects atom by atom. Part of the mystique of this work were his warnings about the dangers of losing control of nanotechnology, especially in the case of unbridled self-replication. These ideas and warnings caught on and nanotech quickly became widely accepted and deliberated upon as a field.

Current commercial applications of nanotechnology are relatively few but are steadily growing, and nano-enabled materials and nanotech processes are finding their way into many manufacturing industries. Nanotech is harnessed in the manufacture of advanced computer chips. Nanotechnology is used to micronize titanium dioxide and zinc oxide to give sunscreen better ultraviolet (UV) protection against the sun and to preclude leaving a visible white film on the skin. Micronized particles and nanoparticles are also used in the production of scratch-proof eyeglasses and stain-repellant paints and fabrics.

A large swathe of cutting-edge nanotechnology remains within the domain of research and development in industries such as ICT, medicine, defense, energy, and aviation. The quest for greater computing power through the miniaturization of MOS transistors helped facilitate advances in nanotechnology. It is rational therefore that nanotechnology holds great promise for computer science as its breakthroughs are applied in building next-generation quantum computers. It could also facilitate the creation of much tinier sensors to be used in greater densities to allow the collection of more information at the micro level for the furtherance of IoT.

In medicine, nanotechnology is being explored particularly for its potential to engender potent drug delivery systems that convey specific quanta of active ingredients only to morbid or affected parts of the body, saving the rest of the body from the side effects of collateral exposure. Nanomedicine may also foster the design of drug encapsulation platforms fashioned to release drugs in a specific or regular frequency.[5]

---

[4] Drexler, K.E. 1986. *Engines of Creation: The Coming Era of Nanotechnology*. NY: Anchor Books, Doubleday.

[5] "Manufacturing at the Nanoscale." Nano.gov.

The advance of nanoscience tools and methods is making it easier to study genes and manipulate DNA. Consequent breakthroughs in genetic engineering may enable us to eliminate erstwhile deadly cancers. DNA robots could be used to target the genetic code of bacteria and infectious pathogens in the body.

In public health, nanotech has potential for the development of cheaper but effective water purification systems. Silver nanoparticles are already being used as antibacterial agents in silver-based air and water filters, textiles, and food packaging.[6]

For manufacturing industries, nanotechnology holds promise for the leaner mass production of certain products as it is very productive yet relatively cost-effective, in terms of energy and raw materials. Nanoscience can also result in new materials and unique substances with special physical properties that are prized by certain industries. Silica nanoparticles, for example, can be used in strengthening carbon fiber. Carbon nanotubes are six times lighter than steel but a hundred times stronger. Carbon nanotubes can be spun into threads to electro-thermally conductive yarns and sheets or cutting-edge structural materials.[7]

Nanotechnology is also being applied to the production of superalloys. Superalloys are special alloys that can withstand extreme temperatures while maintaining strength, stiffness, toughness, and dimensional stability and are thus used in engineering high-temperature parts of jet engines, steam turbines, rockets, and other craft. They also have high resistance to oxidation and corrosion and are typically fashioned from nickel, iron, and/or cobalt in combination with a host of other elements such as titanium and chromium.[8] Prominent superalloys include Incoloy, Inconel, Hastelloy, MP98T, and Waspaloy. The high cost of producing superalloys conventionally is a prohibitive factor in meeting the surging

---

[6] Deshmukh, S.P., S.M. Patil. S.B. Mullani, and S.D. Delekar. 2019. "Silver Nanoparticles as an Effective Disinfectant: A Review." *Materials science & engineering. C, Materials for Biological Applications* 97, 954–965. https://doi.org/10.1016/j.msec.2018.12.102

[7] "Manufacturing at the Nanoscale." *Nano.gov.*

[8] Mouritz, A.P., ed. 2012. *1 - Introduction to Aerospace Materials*, 1–14. Cambridge, UK: Woodhead Publishing. https://doi.org/10.1533/9780857095152.1

demand from aerospace, mobility, and energy industries. Nanotechnology promises to deliver cheaper new methods of making even stronger superalloys. Techniques for synthesizing nanoparticles are being adapted to making superalloys in a new approach called radiolysis,[9] which uses ionization radiation to dissociate molecules.

Nanotech is also important in the energy industries. Scientists are working to develop nanotechnology solutions that will enhance the power and yield of batteries used in electric vehicles, phones, and other devices.

A major benefit of nanoscience is that its progress improves mankind's adeptness at miniaturization. The development of nano tools, equipment, and methodologies makes it easier to miniaturize a host of tasks, activities, and functionalities that in the macro world burden us with bulky equipment and raw materials. The relevance of this is far reaching. Imagine miniaturized air purification systems that are so light that their deployment in space exploration reduces weight on spacecraft and in space suits. Anything that lightens the weight and bulkiness of systems will invariably increase the payload carriable by spacecraft and aircraft, or indeed, by all craft in any of the weight-sensitive industries.

Challenges and Dangers

All scientific breakthroughs are mere tools and can be used to help or harm mankind. Thus, like fire, the blade, and nuclear technology, nanotechnology is a powerful tool that can be used virtuously or maliciously.

Several contemporary activists and groups echo the warnings of K. Eric Drexler in addition to their own other concerns. Unbridled genetic engineering is one of the foremost concerns for certain groups. Some fear that the advent of self-replicating assemblers or nanobots, if not properly regulated, could result in the uncontrollable, exponential growth of *gray goo*, which may cause death or destruction on a massive scale unprecedented

---

[9] Weber, J.H., and M.K. Banerjee. 2016. "Nickel-Based Superalloys: Alloying." Reference Module in *Materials Science and Materials Engineering*. Elsevier. https://doi.org/10.1016/B978-0-12-803581-8.02573-X.

in human history. With the ongoing development of biological nanotech, the fear of gray goo is morphing into fear of a *green goo*.[10]

There are fears about the toxicity of nanoparticles on humans and other lifeforms. The toxicity of substances at the nano level can differ from macro forms and this makes it harder to predict toxicity using macro-level toxicity baselines. There is evidence that nanoparticles can aggregate in the lungs, brains, and nasal passages of rats. Some carbon nanoparticles called buckyballs have also been shown to damage the brains of fish.[11] Indeed, concerns about nanotechnology proliferation in domestic products often revolve around their eventual accumulation into waste systems and ultimately into ecosystems and food chains. The full effects of contaminated waste on aquatic and terrestrial biosystems must be assessed comprehensively.[12]

There are also the more unusual threats to peace and international security. Because of their small scale and fleeting traceability, it is inevitable that nanotechnology will be seized upon by clandestine intelligence services as well as terrorist- or malevolent interests. It is only a matter of time before nanowarfare and nanoattacks become popular terms in international news, just like cyberwarfare. It is up to defense and intelligence communities and international regulatory bodies to create the regulatory frameworks and protocols that will systemize the prevention of the harmful use of nanotechnology and the identification of potential mal actors.

Most of the aforementioned concerns boil down to the fear that surges in nanoscience and nanotechnology could outpace the development of policies to regulate them, and thus result in irremediable damage to society. It is through prompt collaboration among researchers, governments, and public stakeholders that we can create effective frameworks

---

[10] Goo, G. 2004. "The New Nano Threat." *WIRED*, www.wired.com/2004/07/green-goo-the-new-nano-threat/ (accessed July 19, 2004).

[11] Holmes, B. 2004. "Buckyballs Cause Brain Damage in Fish." *NewScientist*, www.newscientist.com/article/dn4825-buckyballs-cause-brain-damage-in-fish/ (accessed March 29, 2004).

[12] Murray, R.G.E. 1993. "A Perspective on S-Layer Research." In *Advances in Bacterial Paracrystalline Surface Layers*, ed. T.J. Beveridge and S.F. Koval, 3–9. US: Springer. https://doi.org/10.1007/978-1-4757-9032-0

to keep this revolutionary technology in check, while still deriving the marked benefits from this groundbreaking new field. But this is easier said than done. Canada's ETC Group has recommended a UN moratorium on nanotech that touches the body.[13] In the United States, similar calls have come from the Centre for Responsible Nanotechnology[14] for the enactment of more balanced and responsible strategies for the global use of nanotech.

3D Printing

3D printing is an additive process for manufacturing three-dimensional objects from digital models or files. In 3D printing, objects are built from the ground up as thin layers of raw material are overlaid on top of one another, until the full three-dimensional object is complete. 3D printing, also known as rapid prototyping, therefore allows the printing of intricate creations of complex design. Additive manufacturing uses much less raw material than its converse, subtractive manufacturing, where objects are sculpted, cut out, or machined from much larger pieces of raw material.

There are different types of 3D printing, each with its merits and demerits, and there are also various raw materials. Raw materials can include ceramics, metal, paper, plastics, concrete and even edible substances such as chocolate or icing. There are seven categories classified by the American Society for Testing and Materials (ASTM).[15]

- **Vat Photopolymerization** employs a vat of resin made of photopolymer that hardens when hit with UV light. This can be done via three methods. Stereolithography (SLA) uses a UV laser to cure a thin layer of the object's cross-section on

[13] "Nanotech Product Recall Underscores Need for Nanotech Moratorium: Is the Magic Gone?" ETC Group, www.etcgroup.org/content/nanotech-product-recall-underscores-need-nanotech-moratorium-magic-gone (accessed April 6, 2006).

[14] http://crnano.org/

[15] ASTM International. 2015. *ISO / ASTM52900-15, Standard Terminology for Additive Manufacturing – General Principles – Terminology.* West Conshohocken, PA: ASTM International, https://doi.org/10.1520/ISOASTM52900-15

the liquid resin surface. Then the cured layer sinks slightly and is coated with more resin to allow another layer to be traced and cured. Digital light processing (DLP) resembles SLA but uses arc lamps or other alternatives to lasers. Continuous liquid interface production (CLIP) is faster than the previous two processes and blasts light unto the transparent bottom of a vat of photosensitive resin, which is lined by an oxygen-permeable membrane. The solidified resin rises very slowly, slow enough for new resin below to harden to it. Thus, the process is continuous, and objects emerge seamlessly out of the resin pool and not in discrete layers.

- **Material Jetting or Inkjet Technology.** This process is akin to the operation of 2D inkjet printers and applies raw material in droplets through a very small nozzle, but in three dimensions. In some cases, UV light is used to cure each printed layer, while in others, the layers harden naturally as they cool.

- **Binder Jetting.** This process also employs jet print heads but, in this case, layers of liquid binder are deposited between layers of powdered raw material to glue them together in the specified dimensions. Unused powder can be saved for reuse.

- **Powder Bed Fusion (PBF).** Here, heat or lasers are used to melt raw material into successive layers. There are several subcategories of PBF. Selective laser sintering (SLS) employs the use of a powerful laser to bind a layer of powder in the required cross-section, and then the layer is lowered for another coating to be deposited above it. Direct metal laser sintering (DMLS) is like SLS except that metal powder is used. Other subcategories include direct metal laser melting (DMLM), multi jet fusion (MJF), and electron beam melting (EBM).

- **Material Extrusion** is a more popular process and utilizes a horizontally mobile arm, armed with a heated nozzle that extrudes polymer down onto a bed that is also vertically mobile. The bed moves down to allow successive layers to be deposited over each other. Chemicals or temperature can be used to fuse layers together. The process is sometimes known as fused deposition modeling (FDM), a term trademarked by Stratasys Inc., the company founded by FDM's inventor, Scott Crump. Alternatively, material extrusion is also known as fused filament fabrication (FFF) because of the plastic filament used by the extrusion nozzle and which is unrolled from spools.

- **Directed Energy Deposition (DED)** is akin to material extrusion but uses an electron beam or laser to melt wire, filament, or powder from metal, polymer, ceramics, or a host of other materials.
- **Sheet Lamination.** This process involves the binding together of sheets of raw material and has two methods. Laminated object manufacturing (LOM) laminates paper and adhesive in alternate layers, while ultrasonic additive manufacturing (UAM) uses ultrasonic welding to bind thin sheets of metal raw material such as titanium or aluminum, which are cut into the required shape.[16]

The 3D Printing Industry

The history of 3D printing is lengthy and varied. In 1950, the American science-fiction author Raymond F. Jones, in his short story *Tools of the Trade*,[17] outlined the concepts behind what he called "molecular spray" and what is now 3D printing or additive manufacturing.

The ensuing three decades saw a few patents describing components or processes akin to modern-day 3D printing being filed by several scientists and inventors. But it was in the 1980s that the concept really took off. Numerous additive methods were developed, and more patents were filed successfully or abandoned, all by the likes of Hideo Kodama, Bill Masters, Alain Le Méhauté, Olivier de Witte, Jean Claude André, Robert

---

[16] "What is 3D Printing?" *3DPrinting.com*, https://3dprinting.com/what-is-3d-printing/ (accessed April 28, 2021).

[17] Jones, R.F. November 1950. "Tools of the Trade." In *Astounding Science Fiction*, ed. J.W. Campbell. NY: Street & Smith Publications, Inc.

Howard, Richard Helinski, Herbert Menhennett, Royden Sanders, James K. McMahon, Steven Zoltan, and Chuck Hull.[18]

From the 1990s, 3D printing technology began to infiltrate major manufacturing industries such as aerospace and automotive and because of costliness, remained mainly in the industrial domain until the 2000s, when the technology became more affordable for the consumer market. Since then, 3D printing has been revolutionizing the way we think of production at home and commercially. Enthusiastic hobbyists are even building their own printers at home or experimenting with pushing the boundaries of what we can do with the tech.

The 3D printing business landscape is dominated by five players. With a revenue (TTM) of $566.6 million and net income (TTM) of -$78.4 million of 3D Systems Corp or DDD is the market leader in the 3D market. 3D Systems was founded in 1986 by Charles W. Hull, who is credited with patenting stereolithography and leading the creation of the SLA 3D printer. The company offers 3D printers, materials, software, and support services.[19]

Proto Labs Inc. (PRLB) comes in at second place with a revenue (TTM) of $451.0 million and net income of $58.6 million, followed by FARO Technologies Inc. (TTM Revenue: $334.7 million), Materialise NV or MTLS (TTM Revenue: $205.3 million) and The ExOne Co. or XONE (TTM Revenue: $52.9 million).[20] Other major players include EOS and Stratasys, two early entrants into the market during the 1980s.

Originally the preserve of large industries, 3D printers have come into the consumer market with many affordable options below a thousand U.S. dollars. For consumers who do not want to buy a full 3D printer, there are online third-party options for printing and shipping 3D printed objects. Users can design their STL files or find objects in databases like Thingiverse.[21]

---

[18] Flynt, J. 2021. "A Detailed History of 3D Printing." *3D Insider*, https://3dinsider.com/3d-printing-history/ (accessed April 28, 2021).

[19] Reiff, N. 2020. "5 Biggest 3D Printing Companies." *Investopedia*, www.investopedia.com/articles/investing/081515/three-biggest-3d-printing-companies.asp (accessed September 9, 2020).

[20] Ibid.

[21] www.thingiverse.com/

Applications of 3D Printing

The current and potential impacts of 3D printing on our man-made world and on businesses are truly extraordinary. The major benefit of 3D printing stems from its additive nature; cost savings, due to lean production unlike subtractive manufacturing where larger proportions of raw materials are wasted. The speed of 3D printing already hastens projects in certain industries by enabling quick migration from concept to prototyping, hence the synonym *rapid prototyping*. As the technology evolves and so also the range of raw materials, more industries will gain from the rapid prototyping and on-demand production capabilities of 3D printing.

Additive manufacturing also allows industries to produce on demand or in small batches and avoid the large minimum production quantities typical of some subtractive manufacturing. This can create tremendous benefits on inventory management, supply chain and logistics.

Another major impact of 3D printing is the democratization of production. The growing arsenal of raw materials that can be used in 3D printing is creating a world where consumers will not have to buy finished goods but rather pay for the 3D files for products and then print them at home. Some printers are already able to print consumer items such as clothes, electronic devices, and layered circuitry. Such a dynamic can impact players operating in the courier services market. 3D printing is a reality and is only gaining more widespread attention. Stakeholders in related or competing industries should ready themselves for this shift.

The shift of manufacturing from large industries to the end user makes easy work of on-demand production in remote locations. This has powerful applications for space exploration and military sectors, where vehicles do not need to carry a large variety of tools and hardware, but rather just the raw material necessary to print them as and when they become necessary. This also applies to other payloads such as satellites, air purification systems, and artificial habitats for planet colonization. In short, 3D printing could completely transform the explorative industries. The U.S. company, Made In Space, Inc. (MIS), is a leader in this field and develops microgravity-capable 3D printers.

CHAPTER 8

Energy

The dilemma we find ourselves faced with in the 21st century is that the bulk of our energy is dirty. From the humble wood fire to the thundering jet engines of an aircraft, most of the power used for utilities and mobility is derived from nonrenewable sources that pollute the atmosphere with greenhouse gases and accelerate climate change, with disastrous consequences for future generations.

But there is light on the horizon. After decades of painstaking evangelism and struggles with institutional inertia from establishments benefiting from dirty energy, scientists and progressive politicians have finally been able to get climate change on the agenda of many governments. Clear agendas and timelines for transitioning to alternative fuels and for reducing carbon footprints are embedded in such frameworks as the Kyoto Protocol, the Paris Agreement, and the UN's Sustainable Development Goals. A global push for alternative clean energy is now real, alive, and kicking.

Like previous industrial revolutions, our upcoming Fourth Industrial Revolution is expected to herald the rise of new forms of energy. In this chapter, we will cover ongoing developments in contemporary energy resources as well as radical new technologies for clean energy generation. It is likely that the future of green power may hinge less on one cure-for-all fuel but lean more on a wider arsenal of clean alternatives, with concomitant improvements to energy transmission, storage, and efficiency.

Clean or renewable energy refers to energy extracted from renewable natural resources and are thus considered healthier for the environment than dirty fossil fuels, even if they are not all without some environmental impacts.

Solar

Solar is the most prominent of alternative energy sources. Yet, it is ironic to note that at the heart of it all, most of the dirty hydrocarbon fuels, vis-a-vis oil and gas, are ultimately solar derived. Crude oil is formed from the decayed multimillion-year-old remains of ancient biological ecosystems, which at their core were founded on plants and phytoplankton, which in turn were nourished by the sun, thereby being solar harvesters. The problem with this form of solar-derived energy is that it flowed through convoluted, and therefore inefficient, carbon-based biological pathways.

For more efficient ways to harness the sun's energy without having to go through long, winding biological pathways over millions of years, solar technologies use synthetic pathways that are relatively instantaneous. As opposed to petroleum, these innovations fix solar energy directly into various media for our use, with less energy loss than that from conversions down a food chain.

Solar power is usually generated by semiconducting materials in photovoltaic (PV) cells that convert sunlight into electricity. Sunlight causes excitement of electrons in the semiconductor, and the resulting current is then either used directly or stored in batteries and other storage systems. Solar energy can also be harvested as direct heat or hot water. For instance, there are passive solar homes that absorb sunlight and warmth through windows but then use concrete, bricks, and other special materials to trap that heat within the house.[1]

Solar power is generally good for the environment because, apart from any pollution lapses during manufacturing, there are no negative effects on the environment because there is no combustion generating any greenhouse gases. Yet, though solar power has the celebrated benefit of being practically endless, its inception was plagued with high upfront installation costs. Nevertheless, as technologies have advanced,

---

[1] "Passive Solar Home Design." *Energy Saver, Energy.gov*, www.energy.gov/energysaver/energy-efficient-home-design/passive-solar-home-design (accessed April 26, 2021).

solar energy solutions have steadily gotten cheaper over the years,[2] making them affordable for working class families and small- to large-scale businesses.

Apart from initial setup costs for cells, batteries, and the like, solar power can supplement or completely supplant traditional energy sources, and potentially eliminate energy bills ... forever. Installation costs are quickly recovered via savings in bills. In some countries, this is helped by the fact that the government subsidizes or incentivizes solar installation costs. In the United States, for instance, some local, state, and federal authorities provide solar investment tax credits or rebates. The UK does something similar with the *Feed-in Tariff*.

Solar power can be generated on a large scale in solar farms or on a small scale via solar panels in homes or neighborhoods. In fact, solar technologies have improved so much that some solar-enabled homes produce excess electricity that homeowners can feed into the public grid for money. Solar solutions are also perfect for remote areas where traditional power utilities are nonexistent.

Emerging Solar Innovations

Solar cells are not as efficient in unideal weather conditions and can be prone to deterioration over exceedingly long periods. Also, domestic solar solutions are usually limited to roof spaces of homes or buildings. There is a new wave of solar innovations that blend form and function in buildings. These building-integrated photovoltaics (BIPV) include solar windows, solar skylights, solar blinds, solar roof shingles, and more. BIPVs can capitalize on the large vertical surface areas of tall buildings and skyscrapers, as well as the smaller surface areas of homes.

Another promising technology is solar-paneled roads. In the 2000s, an American couple, Scott Brusaw and his wife Julie, developed sturdy hexagonal panels that could be used for smart roads.[3] The Federal

---

[2] "Solar." *Energy.gov*, www.energy.gov/science-innovation/energy-sources/renewable-energy/solar (accessed April 26, 2021).

[3] Brusaw, S. 2014. "Solar FREAKIN' Roadways!" YouTube video, www.youtube.com/watch?v=qlTA3rnpgzU (accessed May 19, 2014).

Highway Administration of the United States Department of Transportation (USDOT) awarded them several Small Business Innovation Research (SBIR) grants, which they used to conduct feasibility studies and construct a pilot solar parking lot in Sandpoint, Idaho, in 2016. The Brusaws propose that the 28,000 miles of road in the United States can meet the United States' energy needs three times over.[4] But they are not just depending on public willpower and infrastructure; they are making their solution directly available to individuals to pave their driveways and grounds.[5]

The United States is not the only country experimenting with solar roads. China, which already produces over 75 percent of the world's solar panels, has several functional solar road testbeds. For instance, in the city of Jinan in Shandong Province, two companies—Shandong Pavenergy and Qilu Transportation—are respectively producing and deploying unique polymer panels that exhibit more friction than regular roads. And in France, Canada, and Japan (and the United States), the French civil engineering giant, Colas, has developed over 25 solar parking lots and roads.

The potential advantages of solar roads are monumental. Using existing roads and highways for solar generation could eliminate the costly annexation of prime property for solar farms. The proximity and comprehensive distribution of roads within settlements and city centers means that power will be generated close to the end user and this will preclude massive energy losses through far-flung transmission lines. Durable solar roads could help cities save the money spent in resurfacing roads every few years. Solar roads can also be embedded with light-emitting diodes (LEDs), which can produce on-demand illuminated signage and road markings.[6] Perhaps, dynamic digital road signage could be used to resize

---

[4] Cunningham, N. 2014. "Five Crazy New Forms of Energy That Just Might Work." *OilPrice.com*, https://oilprice.com/Energy/Energy-General/Five-Crazy-New-Forms-Of-Energy-That-Just-Might-Work.html (accessed June 26, 2014).

[5] https://solarroadways.com/

[6] Bradsher, K. 2018. "Free Power from Freeways? China Is Testing Roads Paved with Solar Panels." *The New York Times*, www.nytimes.com/2018/06/11/business/energy-environment/china-solar-roads-renewables.html (accessed June 11, 2018).

or reorder lanes at short notice, in response to changing traffic conditions, to optimize flow.

While the Brusaws are looking at smart roads that generate electricity, other innovators are working on smart roads that wirelessly charge electric vehicles as they pass over them. In Sweden, *Smartroad Gotland*[7] is a 1.6-kilometer test project for in-road inductive charging. This testbed uses copper coils that are wrapped in rubber and buried three inches beneath the road and then connected to the grid. Vehicles must be equipped with special wireless receivers to charge as they ply the road.

Could such dynamic electric vehicle charging (DEVC) solutions be combined with the previously mentioned solar roads? Imagine a future where roadways generate solar power and simultaneously charge the electric vehicles plying them. This would eliminate the need for electric charging stations and make vehicles able to operate practically endlessly.

A similar concept to that of Julie and Scott Brusaw's hexagonal road panels is that of floating solar panels or floatovoltaics, which can be used on certain water bodies.[8] Of course, the choice of waterbodies would need to factor in any possible ecological impacts.[9]

A major problem that solar solutions have is reduced yield during periods of darkness and cloudy weather. Scientists and some governments are looking at overcoming this problem by deploying solar panels in space.[10] This solution entails space solar platforms beaming down their energy to terrestrial base stations via microwaves or lasers. The base stations will then convert the energy for immediate use or stow it in storage

[7] www.smartroadgotland.com/

[8] Bennington-Castro, J. 2019. "Floating Solar Farms: How 'Floatovoltaics' Could Provide Power Without Taking Up Valuable Real Estate." *NBC Universal*, www.nbcnews.com/mach/science/floating-solar-farms-how-floatovoltaics-could-provide-power-without-taking-ncna969091 (accessed February 11, 2019).

[9] Chester, M. 2019. "Floatovoltaics: Clever Innovation or Solution in Search of a Problem?" *Chester Energy and Policy*, https://chesterenergyandpolicy.com/2019/09/19/floatovoltaics-clever-innovation-or-solution-in-search-of-a-problem/ (accessed September 19, 2019).

[10] "Space-Based Solar Power." *Energy.gov*, www.energy.gov/articles/space-based-solar-power (accessed March 6, 2014).

systems.[11] The viability of such solutions will be enhanced by concurrent advances in commercial space transport solutions, some of which are discussed later in Chapter 9. Cheaper options of sending space solar equipment to space may be the critical factor that determines if such systems ever become a commercial reality.

Hydrogen

Hydrogen remains one of the most hyped and promising green energy solutions to combat climate change. Its combustion is powerful and creates nothing but water, and it can also be used to generate power through chemical reactions in fuel cells, producing the same by-products: water and heat.

Hydrogen is the most abundant element in the known universe, but on earth it does not occur in nature on its own but is almost always tied to other elements, like with oxygen to make water. To produce it therefore, it must be extracted from compounds by separating it from other elements. This requires energy and thus diminishes hydrogen's energy efficacy when talking about preventing pollution and climate change. Thus, hydrogen is not an energy source, but when tied with abundant energy from solar and other clean sources, it can act as a potent carrier and deliverer of clean, green power.

Heretofore, hydrogen has primarily been obtained from natural gas. Hydrogen obtained from natural gas is usually called gray hydrogen, but when the carbon dioxide by-product is captured and stored, then the hydrogen is then referred to as blue hydrogen.[12] The production of hydrogen from natural gas generally negates the environmental benefits of hydrogen's clean combustion. Electrolysis—the use of electricity to split water into hydrogen and oxygen—solves this problem but, being more expensive, is not used as widely as natural gas. Hydrogen derived from

---

[11] Cunningham, N. n.d. "Five Crazy New Forms of Energy That Just Might Work."

[12] Magill, J. 2021. "Blue Vs. Green Hydrogen: Which Will the Market Choose?" *Forbes*, www.forbes.com/sites/jimmagill/2021/02/22/blue-vs-green-hydrogen-which-will-the-market-choose/?sh=4326349f3878 (accessed February 22, 2021).

electrolysis that is driven by electricity from renewable energy sources such as solar or wind is called green hydrogen, but when that electricity is from solar only, the output is often termed, yellow hydrogen. Likewise, when hydrogen is produced by electrolysis fueled by electricity from nuclear energy, it is referred to as pink hydrogen.[13]

Emerging Innovations in Hydrogen and Hydrogen Fuel Cells

The International Energy Agency in a milestone report, *The Future of Hydrogen*,[14] calls for the timely leverage of progress in hydrogen-related policies and businesses to expand technologies and reduce costs, and thereby drive hydrogen mass adoption.

Blue hydrogen technologies continue to draw attention from large investors like Breakthrough Ventures, a climate technology fund backed by Bill Gates.[15] Other ventures or start-ups like NuScale are focusing on improving high-temperature electrolysis by harnessing nuclear process heat and to perfect small reactor modules that produce pink hydrogen in higher volumes than solar hydrogen plants, but at comparable costs.[16]

Meanwhile, vigorous research and development efforts continue to yield technological breakthroughs in hydrogen fuel cells that are used in electric vehicles, homes, backup power storage, and more. Hydrogen fuel cells operate similar to batteries and continually produce electricity and heat for as long as hydrogen is supplied. The conversion of chemical to electrical energy in fuel cells can be up to 60-percent efficient, better than

---

[13] Giovannini, S. 2020. "50 Shades of (Grey and Blue and Green) Hydrogen." *Energy Cities*, https://energy-cities.eu/50-shades-of-grey-and-blue-and-green-hydrogen/ (accessed November 13, 2020).

[14] IEA. 2019. *The Future of Hydrogen*. Paris, France: IEA, www.iea.org/reports/the-future-of-hydrogen

[15] Shieber, J. 2021. "A Startup Using a New Tech to Make Hydrogen Extracts Cash from Bill Gates' Climate Tech Fund." *Yahoo! Finance*, https://finance.yahoo.com/news/startup-using-tech-hydrogen-extracts-130103060.html (accessed February 9, 2021).

[16] Delbert, C. 2020. "Tiny Nuclear Reactors Yield a Huge Amount of Clean Hydrogen." *Yahoo! Finance*, https://finance.yahoo.com/news/tiny-nuclear-reactors-yield-huge-200900607.html (accessed December 14, 2020).

regular combustion engines. With lower emissions, and only water as a by-product, they do not contribute to climate change.[17]

Wind

Wind energy involves the conversion of wind flow into electricity, usually through the use of turbines. It is cheap, clean, does not generate waste, and releases no harmful emissions into the environment. Nevertheless, the location of wind solutions in often remote areas places them far from the ultimate end users of the energy, and this necessitates expensive transmission lines covering long distances. Also, some wind turbines generate noise locally and can kill the birds that strike them when in operation. In the United States, wind power made up 6.6 percent of net U.S. electricity generation in 2018.[18] In Europe as a whole, however, wind powers about 15 percent of electricity generation (2020),[19] while in countries like Denmark, wind power accounts for over 95 percent of the country's electricity needs (2017).[20]

Emerging Innovations in Wind Energy

One growing pursuit in wind energy circles today is high-altitude wind power.[21] This solution may comprise of wind turbines installed on floating airship-, balloon-, kite-, or kytoon-like platforms, which will operate at heights where air currents are powerful and dependable. Flying wind farms will be advantageous because of increased yields; winds can be twice

---

[17] "Fuel Cells." *Energy.gov*, www.energy.gov/eere/fuelcells/fuel-cells (accessed April 26, 2021).
[18] "Renewable Energy." *C2ES*, www.c2es.org/content/renewable-energy/ (accessed April 26, 2021).
[19] "Wind Power Is Already 15% of Europe's Electricity." *reve*, www.evwind.es/2020/03/03/wind-power-is-already-15-of-europes-electricity/73883 (accessed March 3, 2020).
[20] "Wind, The Best Commitment to our Future." *Iberdrola*, www.iberdrola.com/environment/wind-power-evolution-europe (accessed April 26, 2021).
[21] Cunningham, N. n.d. "Five Crazy New Forms of Energy That Just Might Work."

as fast at high altitude and with eight times more power density. Flying wind turbines would eliminate the need for costly concrete foundations and other infrastructure, which underpin land-based and offshore wind. They would also cause less bird deaths.[22]

Numerous companies are currently working on this solution and the technology shows promise. One such company is Massachusetts-based Altaeros Energies,[23] winner of the 2011 ConocoPhillips Energy Prize,[24] with its Airborne Wind Turbine encased in an inflatable helium shell, which is designed to operate above a thousand feet. Demonstrations at just 350 feet produced twice the power of a tower-mounted turbine.[25]

Tidal and Wave Power

Tidal and wave energy technologies harness power from mass movements of oceans, seas, and large water bodies. The ebb and flow of tides and the rise and fall of waves are potent and reliable sources of clean alternative energy and generate no waste; however, the technologies to utilize them are relatively fledgling. They can thus be fairly costly; and this can slow their widespread adoption. In a typical example, rising costs resulted in the premature cancellation of a wave power initiative in Oregon by the company, Ocean Power Technologies, despite state and federal support and grants.[26]

---

[22] Craighill, C. n.d. "The Wind Turbine Rises: Is High-Altitude the Future of Wind Energy?" *Greenpeace*, www.greenpeace.org/usa/wind-turbine-rises-high-altitude-future-wind-energy/

[23] www.altaeros.com/ (accessed July 2, 2014).

[24] "ConocoPhillips, Penn State Energy Prize for Airborne Wind Turbines." *Penn State News, The Pennsylvania State University*, https://news.psu.edu/story/154159/2011/10/26/conocophillips-penn-state-energy-prize-airborne-wind-turbines (accessed October 26, 2011).

[25] Altaeros. n.d. "Altaeros - Airborne Wind Turbine Prototype 2012." YouTube video, www.youtube.com/watch?v=rsHUALU--Wc (accessed April 19, 2012).

[26] Schwartz, D. 2014. "Wave Energy Developer Pulls Plug on Oregon Project." *OPB*, www.opb.org/news/article/wave-energy-developer-pulls-plug-on-oregon-project/ (accessed March 6, 2014).

Yet, efforts continue to tap this virtually limitless power source. October 2020 saw the deployment in the New York City's East River of three tidal turbines developed by the company, Verdant Power.[27] This demonstration project that counts as the first licensed tidal power initiative in the United States is showing remarkable results; it generated 100 MWh within its first 85 days, quicker than expected.[28]

Some companies are even ignoring water's mechanical power and focusing on its thermal properties to generate energy. Lockheed Martin, for instance, has developed a thermodynamic heat system that harnesses the temperature differential between frigid deep water and warmer surface water to drive an ammonia steam cycle: a process called Ocean Thermal Energy Conversion (OTEC).[29] The company is working to develop a pilot 5- to 10-megawatt floating plant off the shores of Hawaii and is even partnering with Hong Kong-based Reignwood in a joint venture to build the world's largest OTEC power plant in the high seas of southern China.[30]

Geothermal

Geothermal power is generated from heat captured from the earth's crust. This can be done by pumping water underground to be heated

---

[27] "Three Verdant Power Tidal Turbines Deployed in New York City's East River." *EE Online*, https://electricenergyonline.com/article/energy/category/hydro/86/875110/three-verdant-power-tidal-turbines-deployed-in-new-york-city-s-east-river.html (accessed January 11, 2021).

[28] "New Report Shows Marine Energy Has Potential to Power 220 Million U.S. Homes." *National Hydropower Association*, www.globenewswire.com/news-release/2021/03/15/2193113/0/en/New-Report-Shows-Marine-Energy-Has-Potential-to-Power-220-Million-U-S-Homes.html (accessed March 15, 2021).

[29] "Lockheed Testing the Waters for Ocean Thermal Energy System." *Energy.gov*, www.energy.gov/articles/lockheed-testing-waters-ocean-thermal-energy-system (accessed May 27, 2010).

[30] Sharda. 2019. "World's Largest Ocean Thermal Energy Conversion (OTEC) Power Plant to Come Up in China." *Marine Insight*, www.marineinsight.com/offshore/worlds-largest-ocean-thermal-energy-conversion-otec-power-plant-to-come-up-in-china/ (accessed December 11, 2019).

and converted to steam by the earth's heat and then harnessing this steam to move a turbine generator. Geothermal energy can also be harnessed directly for heating. Geothermal power is attractive because it has little impact on surface-based ecosystems and is virtually limitless. However, like tidal and wave power, its development is currently expensive, and this is a disincentive when compared to other alternative energy solutions.

Nevertheless, geothermal energy holds amazing promise, with the World Bank estimating that about 40 countries around the world have enough geothermal resources to meet most—if not all—of their energy needs at relatively lower costs.[31] In the United States, geothermal resources are concentrated in western states.

A current trend in geothermal power is *GeoExchange* heating and cooling; a class of solutions that can use the steady temperature of the ground several feet down to stabilize the temperature of a house, regardless of season. They are sometimes called ground source heat pumps (GSHPs) or geothermal heat pumps (GHPs). In the United States, GeoExchange systems can be more expensive to set up than regular heating, ventilation, and air conditioning (HVAC) alternatives, but can save costs in the long run over a 3- to 10-year horizon, or even if one capitalizes on state and federal incentives or tax credits.[32]

Nuclear

In the quest for clean alternative power, nuclear power is still receiving a lot of attention. Nuclear fission, which is behind traditional nuclear solutions, is clean and efficient but has extremely catastrophic consequences when accidental meltdowns occur, such as the infamous accidents at the Three Mile Island (Pennsylvania, U.S.), Chernobyl (Ukraine, USSR), and Fukushima Daiichi (Japan) nuclear power plants in 1979, 1986, and

[31] "Geothermal Energy is on a Hot Path." *The World Bank*, www.worldbank. org/en/news/feature/2018/05/03/geothermal-energy-development-investment (accessed May 3, 2018).
[32] "GeoExchange Systems (Ground Source Heat Pumps)." https://files.dep.state. pa.us/Air/AirQuality/AQPortalFiles/Advisory%20Committees/CCAC/Docs/ GeoExchange_Heating_and_Cooling_final_version.pdf

2011, respectively. A statistical study by Rose and Sweeting in 2016[33] assessed past nuclear core melt accidents and deduced *a failure rate of 1 per 3704 reactor years*, a result suggestive of another accident within a decade. Nuclear fission also generates dangerous radioactive waste, which is cumbersome to store or dispose of.

Researchers are currently looking at alternative nuclear solutions that are powerful yet bear no risk of runaway nuclear reactions and explosions. Nuclear fusion is the converse good twin of nuclear fission and is the same process that powers our sun. In a nutshell, the process of nuclear fusion is the fusion of two or more atomic nuclei to form one or more new atomic nuclei with a release or absorption of energy. Attempts to develop nuclear fusion energy solutions are generally aimed at fusing two atoms of hydrogen to form helium, with a release of energy. There are two schools of thought as to how to achieve this: hot fusion and cold fusion.

Hot fusion would essentially entail the heating of hydrogen fuel to about 100 million degrees Celsius (or 180 million degrees Fahrenheit) to form a plasma before the atoms will begin to fuse.[34] This heating of the universe's most abundant element (70 percent of all matter)[35] into the universe's most common state of matter (99 percent of the visible universe) is expected to yield an incredible amount of almost inexhaustible power, without the production of dangerous, resilient radioactive waste.

The main challenge with hot fusion is how to maintain plasma stably and under pressure long enough to achieve ignition, which is when the fusion reaction becomes self-sustaining. The energy yield of such a

---

[33] Rose, T., and T. Sweeting. 2016. "How Safe is Nuclear Power? A Statistical Study Suggests Less Than Expected." *Bulletin of the Atomic Scientists* 72, no. 2, 112–115, www.tandfonline.com/doi/full/10.1080/00963402.2016.1145910

[34] Parfit, P. 2021. "Future Power: Where Will the World Get Its Next Energy Fix?" *National Geographic*, www.nationalgeographic.com/environment/article/powering-the-future (accessed April 26, 2021).

[35] Siegel, E. 2020. "This Is Where The 10 Most Common Elements in The Universe Come From." *Forbes*, www.forbes.com/sites/startswithabang/2020/05/25/this-is-where-the-10-most-common-elements-in-the-universe-come-from/?sh=696452cdd24b (accessed May 25, 2020).

self-sustaining nuclear fusion reaction is projected to be about four times that of typical nuclear fission reactions.[36]

The in vogue nuclear fusion model is the tokamak, which forms the heart of the International Thermonuclear Experimental Reactor (ITER),[37] a massive 35-nation project in southern France to prove the feasibility of fusion and which aims for first plasma in 2025 and sustainable ignition by 2035. A tokamak uses strong electric currents and magnetic fields to contain and heat the fuel into plasma, a process called magnetic confinement fusion (MCF).[38]

Other trending efforts at nuclear fusion are leaning toward smaller reactors that also harness the power of magnets to compress fuel into hot plasma. General Fusion is a Canadian nuclear fusion company backed by major investors including Jeff Bezos and Tobias Lutke (founder of Shopify). General Fusion is developing a magnetized target fusion (MTF) reactor that will use pistons to pressurize fuel into superhot plasma and constrain that plasma within a powerful magnetic field. A rival company in the United States, Commonwealth Fusion Systems, which is backed by firms set up by investors like Bill Gates is working on similar technology, which will harness a 10-ton superconducting magnet to contain and pressurize the hydrogen fuel.[39]

Not to be left out, Google is funding research efforts to reassess the concept of cold fusion. Cold fusion is a controversial prospect in scientific circles, with some believing it is entirely possible and others dismissing it as superstition. Cold fusion is the hypothetical attainment of nuclear fusion at low (or room) temperatures. Martin Fleischmann and Stanley Pons, both United States-based chemists, claimed at a press conference in

[36] "Nuclear Fusion Power." *World Nuclear Association*, www.world-nuclear.org/information-library/current-and-future-generation/nuclear-fusion-power.aspx (accessed February 2021).

[37] www.iter.org/proj/inafewlines

[38] Apte, P. 2020. "Tokamak, the Promise of Magnetic Fusion." *ENI*, www.eni.com/en-IT/scientific-research/tokamak-promise-magnetic-fusion.html (accessed November 17, 2020).

[39] Delbert, C. 2021. "Jeff Bezos Is Backing an Ancient Kind of Nuclear Fusion." *Yahoo! Finance*, https://finance.yahoo.com/news/jeff-bezos-backing-ancient-kind-202600988.html (accessed January 25, 2021).

March 1989[40] that they had successfully achieved cold fusion by passing an electric current through two palladium plates in deuterium-rich *heavy water*. Unfortunately, enthusiastic independent efforts to repeat and verify their experiment yielded conflicting results. Even two reviews by the U.S. Department of Energy found no conclusive evidence of their claims of cold fusion.[41] The topic has remained a controversial one ever since.

Some scientists have held on to and still believe in the plausibility of cold fusion, which is now commonly referred to as low-energy nuclear reactions (LENR). Google's project to reassess several historical cold fusion claims has so far found no evidence that it is possible; however, the team has achieved other related breakthroughs in material science and pioneered new measurement techniques. Google has spent over $10 million on the project since 2015, but is also investing in the more orthodox fusion research efforts of companies like TAE technologies.[42]

Energy Storage, Distribution, and Management

Clean energy generation is just one part of the solution to sustainable clean energy for the future. When demand is low, not all the energy generated from renewable sources can be utilized instantaneously. Thus, excess power must be stored for when demand peaks in future. The continual development of powerful energy storage technologies therefore is critical to complement the sourcing of clean power.

Small-scale storage systems rely heavily on lithium-ion battery technology, but when it comes to large-scale energy storage, pumped hydro is still the current market leader, accounting for 95 percent of the world's

---

[40] Krivit, S. 2011. "1989 - March 23 - Cold Fusion Press Conference at University of Utah." YouTube video, www.youtube.com/watch?v=6CfHaeQo6oU&t=25s (accessed April 25, 2011).

[41] Gibney, E. 2019. "Google Revives Controversial Cold-Fusion Experiments." *Nature*, www.nature.com/articles/d41586-019-01683-9 (accessed May 27, 2019).

[42] Greshko, M. 2019. "Cold Fusion Remains Elusive—But These Scientists May Revive the Quest." *National Geographic*, www.nationalgeographic.com/science/article/cold-fusion-remains-elusive-these-scientists-may-revive-quest (accessed May 29, 2019).

storage capacity.[43] Yet, a range of alternative energy storage systems are in development. In the United States, Primus Power, for example, is pioneering several advances in *low-cost, long-duration energy storage* to enable the establishment of *self-sufficient, high-resilience micro-grids*.[44] Their Energy Pod 2 flow battery harnesses chemical reactions in a flowing electrolyte to store or supply electricity and can be set up in a pack of six within a standard 8 × 40-foot ISO shipping container, while providing peak power of 25 kW and energy storage of 125 kW at 70-percent efficiency.

In some countries, homes powered by wind or solar can resupply their excess electricity to power companies or other users through the main electrical grid, and get paid for it. To improve efficiency and distribution, governments will have to modernize their grids by making them smart. Artificial intelligence, 5G, IoT, blockchain, and quantum computing are all emerging tools that can be harnessed to improve the responsiveness of centralized national grids and modular community-based microgrids, making them self-optimizing. Blockchain in particular is well-suited for transparently mediating the autonomous peer-to-peer trade of domestically produced electricity between consumers, and for optimizing energy usage in real time. The Brooklyn Microgrid[45] is a landmark community-based project where prosumers can trade power using blockchain tech.

As grid parity is achieved and renewable energy sources become cheaper and more efficient than regular nonrenewable sources, the economic benefits of smart—sometimes prosumer-driven—energy will drive universal access to energy, even in remote regions. It will quickly become futile to keep innovating technologies for harnessing dirty fuels, which poison our ground, air, and water resources, and cause irreparable losses of biodiversity.

---

[43] Deign, J. 2020. "Pumped Hydro Moves to Retain Storage Market Leadership." *Greentech Media*, www.greentechmedia.com/articles/read/pumped-hydro-moves-to-retain-storage-market-leadership (accessed November 4, 2020).

[44] Primus Power. 2017. "How Advances in Long-Duration, Low-Cost Energy Storage are Making Possible the Creation of Self-Sufficient, High-Resilience Micro-Grids." https://primuspower.com/assets/pdf/Self-Sufficient-High-Resilience-Micro-Grids.pdf (accessed August 2017).

[45] www.brooklyn.energy/

CHAPTER 9

Mobility

The impacts of the Fourth Industrial Revolution are all-pervasive, touching every aspect of modern-day society. The field of mobility is no exception. Transportation industries and technologies are being fundamentally reimagined and redesigned to engender functionality and deliver the basic impetus: safe, fast mobility. A few key trending transport technologies and concepts are covered in this chapter.

Autonomous Vehicles and Driverless Technologies

The 2020s promise to exciting times in the fields of autonomous vehicles (AVs) and driverless technologies. There are many reasons that driverless technologies are receiving so much attention from the public and private sectors. One of the major rationales for driverless mobility is simply the need to save lives.

Road carnage claims the lives of over 1.35 million victims worldwide every year, which is approximately 3,700 a day. In the United States, traffic accidents are the primary cause of death for people aged below 55, while across the globe they are the leading cause of death for people aged 5 to 29.[1] These statistics represent a massive loss of human life with calamitous ripple effects on affected families or loved ones, and on injured survivors. The impacts of such human capital losses on global economies are unquantifiable, especially for low- to middle-income countries, which account for over 90 percent of the yearly casualties.

---

[1] "Road Traffic Injuries and Deaths—A Global Problem." *Centers for Disease Control and Prevention, National Center for Injury Prevention and Control*, www.cdc.gov/injury/features/global-road-safety/index.html (accessed December 14, 2020).

The causes of road accidents are chiefly related to human error, stemming from tiredness, driving under the influence (DUI), distractions, and more.[2] This is where driverless technologies find relevance, because when perfected, they could foster safer transport systems that are not dependent on the vigilance and skill of drivers.

Another driver of autonomous mobility is the push for more efficient traffic flows. According to INRIX, a recognized authority on transportation analytics, road congestion costed the United States economy about $88 billion in 2019.[3] The INRIX Global Traffic Scorecard also estimates that the United Kingdom lost 6.9 billion pounds in 2019 from road congestion.[4] Studies have shown that a lot of traffic congestion is caused simply by lags in driver perception and reaction time,[5] leading to a phenomenon called phantom traffic jams.[6] Driverless cars navigated by centralized traffic control networks could eliminate the need for the variable buffer zones that human drivers keep between vehicles to maintain braking distances and which often contribute to phantom traffic jams on roadways.

Centralized traffic navigation could seamlessly move swarms of vehicles en masse with minimal intervehicle spacing, such that they move like the tethered cars of a train. Such networks would also be instantaneously

[2] Stanton, N., and P. Salmon. 2009. "Human Error Taxonomies Applied to Driving: A Generic Driver Error Taxonomy and Its Implications For Intelligent Transport Systems." *Safety Science* 47, 227–237. https://doi.org/10.1016/j.ssci.2008.03.006

[3] "INRIX: Congestion Costs Each American Nearly 100 hours, $1,400 A Year." *INRIX*, https://inrix.com/press-releases/2019-traffic-scorecard-us/ (accessed March 9, 2020).

[4] "INRIX Global Traffic Scorecard: Congestion cost UK economy £6.9 billion in 2019." *Automotive World*, www.automotiveworld.com/news-releases/inrix-global-traffic-scorecard-congestion-cost-uk-economy-6-9-billion-in-2019/ (accessed March 9, 2020).

[5] Lizbetin, J., and B. Ladislav. 2017. "The Influence of Human Factor on Congestion Formation on Urban Roads," *Procedia Engineering* 187, 206–211. https://doi.org/10.1016/j.proeng.2017.04.366

[6] Metcalfe, T. 2018. "'Phantom' Traffic Jams Are Real — and Scientists Know How to Stop Them." *Live Science*, www.livescience.com/61862-why-phantom-traffic-jams-happen.html (accessed February 26, 2018).

responsive to changes in road conditions or unforeseen events and could seamlessly redistribute traffic to ensure efficient flow. Fluid traffic flows and leaner navigation enabled by driverless technologies and smart, centralized navigation could drastically reduce energy consumption by precluding inefficient routes and reducing or eliminating waiting times at traffic signals.

In the quest for driverless technology, there have been discrepancies with definitions of terminology such as automated, autonomous, assisted driving, cooperative driving, and others. In 2014, SAE International (formerly, the Society of Automotive Engineers) published a six-level classification scheme called *J3016: Taxonomy and Definitions for Terms Related to On-Road Motor Vehicle Automated Driving Systems.*[7] This system outlines an incremental progression of technologies graduating from *no automation* (level 0) to *full automation* (level 5) in six steps, providing the basis for a standardized approach to automated driving systems.

In the past two decades, a host of companies have ventured into the self-driving market, developing and/or testing models with various levels of autonomy. These companies include Apple, Yandex, Waymo, Uber, and Tesla. Results from millions of miles of tests around the world have been great—depending on whom you speak to[8]—but not without accidents, some of them fatal.[9] It will likely be some time before truly autonomous driving technologies mature and before most people can trust them with their very lives. Regulators and developers of the technology will have to continue to liaise closely until the benefits of a perfected autonomous paradigm are realized. The transformation of global road systems may also require unprecedented shifts in urban planning, connectivity, surveillance, policing, and, of course, law and insurance.

---

[7] "Taxonomy and Definitions for Terms Related to On-Road Motor Vehicle Automated Driving Systems J3016_201401." SAE International, www.sae.org/standards/content/j3016_201401/ (accessed January 16, 2014).

[8] Stewart, E. 2019. "Self-Driving Cars Have to Be Safer Than Regular Cars. The Question Is How Much." *Vox,* www.vox.com/recode/2019/5/17/18564501/self-driving-car-morals-safety-tesla-waymo (accessed May 17, 2019).

[9] Schmelzer, R. 2019. "What Happens When Self-Driving Cars Kill People?" *Forbes,* www.forbes.com/sites/cognitiveworld/2019/09/26/what-happens-with-self-driving-cars-kill-people/?sh=50e38028405c (accessed September 26, 2019).

Drones and Unmanned Vehicles

After decades of lingering within the domain of science-fiction films and folklore, drones have landed firmly into reality. Drones are unmanned craft that operate autonomously or are controlled remotely without the pilot or driver on board. Drones include unmanned aircraft, unmanned aerial vehicles (UAVs), or unmanned aerial systems (UASs), and can also refer to unmanned craft that operate in water or on land.

Drones are remarkable innovations in that their impacts can be incredibly significant. Unmanned aerial vehicles, for example, remove human pilots from the equation and disqualify the use of costly, manned helicopters or planes, making certain operations cheaper and swifter to execute. The exclusion of an onboard pilot also eliminates expensive life support systems and the biological constraints necessitating regular returns to a base. This means that drones, if powered sufficiently, can operate perpetually.

The removal of the human element also suits drones for hazardous tasks, thereby minimizing loss of life and the quanta of financial losses when accidents occur. Invariably, this drives the prominent use of drones in military, defense, and public sector applications. Drones are used in research and development as well as in active combat operations. The large budgets of militaries enable the uninhibited development of various applications for the technology. The Predator drone of the United States, for instance, costs upward of $4 million. Worldwide, the military drone market is expected grow to about $23.78 billion in 2027.[10]

The capability of some drones to operate remotely and continuously over long periods is prized by industries that demand continuous

---

[10] Fortune Business Insights. November 2020. "Military Drone Market Size, Share & COVID-19 Impact Analysis, By Product Type (Fixed Wing, Hybrid and Rotary Wing), By Range (Visual Line of Sight (VLOS), Extended Visual Line of Sight (EVLOS), and Beyond Line of Sight (BLOS)), By Technology (Remotely Operated Drones, Semi-Autonomous Drones, and Autonomous Drones), By Application (Intelligence, Surveillance Reconnaissance and Targeting (ISRT), Combat Operations, Battle Damage Management, Logistics & Transportation and Others), and Regional Forecast, 2020–2027." Report ID: FBI102181, www.fortunebusinessinsights.com/toc/military-drone-market-102181

inspection and monitoring, industries such as aviation and shipping. They enable the autonomous monitoring of warehouses to enhance the accuracy and efficiency of inventory control. Drones can inspect thousands of acres of warehouse or port space and verify the availability of slots, thereby speeding up operations. Some ship operators like Maersk are even testing the use of drones to supply undocked ships at sea.[11] Efforts are also underway to develop drones specifically for monitoring ships and detecting problems or damage. The monitoring capabilities of drones can be extended to farms, construction sites, and even large equipment. Drones are used in the inspection, monitoring, and automated fertilizing of crop fields.

Drones can access remote locations quickly and accurately with minimum human capital, increasing efficiency and often productivity. This makes them perfect for emergency services and disaster management where they can be equipped with thermal sensors to locate missing people in the night as well as in the day. Drones can also be invaluable for traffic monitoring, law enforcement, and border control. They can be used by geographical industries for the mapping of unfriendly terrain and remote locals or by meteorological services for the tracking of storms, tornadoes, hurricanes, and weather events. The media and entertainment industries are big users of drone technologies for aerial photography and so on.

Many drone makers are improving the cargo-carrying capabilities of drones (Figure 9.1) and several notable companies are developing drone technologies to enhance their offerings. Amazon has secured several patents for drone tech including floating blimps or warehouses, which can dispatch drones for deliveries. Google and other online retail stores are also working to develop working models of delivery drones.

Home delivery is still going through the rigors of navigating regulations by the United States Federal Aviation Administration (FAA) and other related public authorities. So far, the FAA is working with eight companies—Wing, Airbus, Amazon, T-Mobile, OneSky, AirMap, Skyward, and Intel—to design the technical specifications for drones to

---

[11] Brandom, R. 2016. "Maersk Just Made the First Official Drone Delivery to an Undocked Ship." *The Verge*, www.theverge.com/2016/3/8/11181756/maersk-drone-delivery-shipping-tanker-nautical (accessed March 8, 2016).

Figure 9.1 Cargo drone concept model by SkyDrive

Credit: SkyDrive

transmit their identity, location, and headings through a mandatory protocol called Remote ID. This tracking system will enable the management of drone air traffic to avoid manned air traffic and other obstacles.[12]

While home delivery of food and other items via drone is still receiving scrutiny form the FAA, the delivery of essential medical supplies is not. Alphabet's drone subsidiary, Wing, was the first entity to be approved by the FAA for drone deliveries. During the Covid-19 pandemic, Wing worked with Walgreens to deliver medicines to customers in quarantine. Also, in the United States, CVS Pharmacy has partnered with UPS to use drones for medical deliveries to The Villages, a retirement community in Florida. The company Zipline is using drones to speed up the transport of medical supplies in North Carolina, Rwanda, and Ghana.[13]

Apart from military, public sector, and commercial applications, drones also find widespread use in the consumer market, where individuals use them for their hobbies or private occupations.

---

[12] Boyle, A. 2020. "Amazon and T-Mobile will help the FAA Design Remote ID Drone Tracking System." *GeekWire*, www.geekwire.com/2020/amazon-t-mobile-will-take-part-faas-remote-id-drone-monitoring-program/ (accessed May 6, 2020).

[13] Banker, S. 2020. "Is the Future of Drones Now?" www.forbes.com/sites/steve-banker/2020/06/11/is-the-future-of-drones-now/?sh=2c2351db3284 (accessed June 11, 2020).

Since 2018 when the market stood at $4.4 billion, the global drone services market has experienced a compound annual growth rate (CAGR) of 55.9 percent and is projected to grow to $63.6 billion by 2025. This represents a potential goldmine for ventures looking to enter the sector.[14]

Generations of Drones

A host of technologies make drones possible: a few of them being artificial intelligence (AI), high-speed wireless connectivity, and computer vision. Some experts in the drone industry like the Amazon Services affiliate air-dronecraze classify seven generations of drones[15] with most conventional drones being fifth- and sixth-generation ones.[16]

First-generation drones feature all types of simple remote-controlled aircraft. Second- and third-generation drones feature static designs, but generation-2 have fixed camera mounts, capture photos and videos, and are piloted manually, while generation-3 come with two-axis gimbals, capture video in high definition, and assisted piloting and simple safety modes.

Fourth- and fifth-generation drones feature transformative designs with generation-4 having three-axis gimbals, 1080P HD video, advanced safety modes, and autopilot modes, while generation-5 feature 360-degree gimbals, 4K HD video, and intelligent piloting modes.

Generation six and seven are suitable for commercial applications and therefore come in designs compliant with regulatory and safety standards, and also feature automated safety modes. They also come with varying levels of platform and payload adaptability (gen-6) or interchangeability

---

[14] Research and Markets. April 2019. "Drone Service Market Application (Aerial Photography, Data Acquisition, Analytics), Industry (Infrastructure, Media & Entertainment, Agriculture), Type (Drone Platform Service, Drone MRO, Drone Training, Solution, Region - Global Forecast to 2025," Report ID: 4763830, www.researchandmarkets.com/r/bgy35s

[15] "The Future of Drone Technology." *Air Drone Craze*, https://airdronecraze.com/drone-tech/ (accessed April 26, 2021).

[16] "Drone Technology Uses and Applications for Commercial, Industrial and Military Drones in 2021 and the Future." *Business Insider*, www.businessinsider.com/drone-technology-uses-applications?IR=T (accessed January 12, 2021).

(gen-7), airspace awareness, intelligent (gen-6), or enhanced (gen-7) piloting models, full autonomy and auto action (gen-7) of launch (take-off), mission execution and return (landing) operations.

Generation-7 drones are already in development. The smart drone Solo by 3DRobotics[17] fulfills all gen-7 requirements and comes enhanced with self-monitoring using smart sensors. Some industry players like Jeff Bezos already stipulate that the development of generation-8 is also underway.[18]

Jetpacks

Another machine that is seeing improvement in recent days is the jetpack. These inventions from science fiction have been developed in various types and forms over the decades and used in a limited way for a variety of purposes. They are compact jet devices typically secured to one's back to thrust the pilot through the air or through space. They have been called by many names through the years, including rocket pack, jet belt, jump belt, and rocket belt. In space exploration, jetpacks or Manned Maneuvering Units are used for untethered spacewalks and short extravehicular excursions into open space. These units are secured to the back of space suits.

Jetpacks for use on earth must overcome the earth's gravity, the weight and drag of the pilot, and may or may not come with flight surfaces. Jetpacks may be tethered or untethered. The jet propellant can be gas or any form of fluid. Through the years, propellants have included oxygen–methane mixes, hydrogen peroxide, compressed nitrogen, and aviation jet fuel. Jetpacks propelled by turbojet engines have shown greater efficiency, power, and flight time, although their engineering can be complex and costly.

One of the most popular jetpacks is the winged jetpack developed by Yves Rossy (Figure 9.2), a Swiss pilot with military and commercial

---

[17] https://3drobotics.com/
[18] Robertson, A. 2014. "Amazon Already Designing Eighth Generation of Delivery Drones, Says Jeff Bezos." *The Verge*, www.theverge.com/2014/4/10/5601992/amazon-designing-eighth-generation-of-delivery-drones-says-jeff-bezos, (accessed April 10, 2014).

Figure 9.2 Yves Rossy and his winged jetpack

Credit: Courtesy of Yves Rossy

experience. The pack features wings of carbon fiber and four miniature turbojet engines that run on kerosene. In September 2008, Rossy (sometimes called *Jetman*) flew a jetpack and conquered the English Channel, flying from France (Calais) to Dover in just over nine minutes, reaching speeds of up to 300 kilometers per hour. He has since achieved other public feats like the Grand Canyon, an appearance in the 18th season of the car show, Top Gear, and a formation flight with an Airbus A380 operated by Emirates Airline.

Other eminent jetpacks are the wingless, *true* backpack-like jetpacks JB-9 (Figure 9.3), JB-10, and JB-11 by the revolutionary company, Jet-Pack Aviation;[19] the Flyboard Air, a jet-powered hoverboard upon which an operator stands; and the Daedalus Flight Pack. Developed by Richard Browning (Gravity Industries), the Daedalus Flight Pack—an *Iron Man*-like device—is an exoskeleton featuring two attached jets and additional jets that can be worn on the operator's arms. There are also a variety of hydro-powered jetpacks, notably the JetLev and Flyboard. These hydro jetpacks are driven by large volumes of fluid supplied externally via a tethered hose.

---

[19] https://jetpackaviation.com/jetpacks/

Figure 9.3 The JB-9 jetpack in flight near the Statue of Liberty

Credit: JetPack Aviation

The Future of Jetpacks

As jetpack technologies continue to evolve through the efforts of commercial entities and hobbyists, it is certain that their applications will keep growing. Already, jetpacks are used in the government or public sphere for space exploration and firefighting. Emergency medical services are ideal candidates to adopt jetpacks for locating and reaching stranded casualties in rough or mountainous terrain.

Flying Cars

Like the jetpack, another staple of science-fiction folklore—the flying car—is seeing steady development in diverse efforts across the world. Conceptual designs and working prototypes are too many to elaborate within this chapter, so we will only mention a few.

Kitty Hawk,[20] an American start-up backed by Larry Page (cofounder of Google), developed a well-popularized personal aircraft called the Kitty Hawk Flyer in 2018. The Flyer is a single-pilot ultra-light electric vehicle powered by eight propellers, which gave it electric vertical takeoff and landing (eVTOL) capability. With more than 25,000 test flights, the Flyer was retired by the company after it had gained all the critical design, testing, handling, and user data it needed for use on developing its future aircraft.[21] The company is currently focusing on two other offerings: the *Wisk* (formerly the *Cora*), an air-taxi; and the *Heavyside*, a powerful, quick, but quiet eVTOL aircraft.

Another radical flying car concept is the SD-03 (Figure 9.4) by the Japanese Toyota-backed company, SkyDrive.[22] It does not have road-plying capability but is a lovely, compact personal air vehicle comparable in size to an automobile and is capable of vertical takeoff and landing (VTOL) door-to-door mobility, without the use of airports. The proto-type first flew in August 2020 and the company plans to release commercial models in 2023.[23] Their design for another upcoming model, currently designated the SD-XX (Figure 9.5), is even more impressive.

China has also entered the fray in a big way. The Guangzhou-based company, Ehang, is a major player in the autonomous aerial vehicle (AAV) market, targeting both passenger transportation and logistics plat-forms. The company initially focused on manned single-seat quadcopter drones but has gone on to develop a two-seat AAV with eight propellers: the Ehang 216.[24] The 216 was first tested in China in 2017 but has since received permits from several international aviation agencies, including

---

[20] https://kittyhawk.aero/

[21] O'Kane, S. 2020. "Kitty Hawk Abandons its Flyer Project, Lays Off Dozens." *The Verge*, www.theverge.com/2020/6/4/21280676/kitty-hawk-cancels-flyer-evtol-drone-aircraft-hoverboke-layoffs (accessed June 4, 2020).

[22] http://en.skydrive2020.com/air-mobility/

[23] Brooks, K.J. 2020. "Toyota-Backed Startup has Flown—and Landed—A Flying Car." *CBS News*, www.cbsnews.com/news/flying-car-test-pilot-skydrive-japan/ (accessed September 29, 2020).

[24] https://evtol.news/ehang-216/

Figure 9.4 The SkyDrive SD-03 in flight

Credit: Courtesy of SkyDrive

the Civil Aviation Authority of Norway,[25] Transport Canada Civil Aviation (TCCA),[26] and Civil Aviation Authority of Austria.[27] The Ehang 216 has even been flown in Amsterdam by Pieter Christiaan, a Dutch prince. Ehang was listed on the Nasdaq Stock Market in 2019.[28] The company has established many strategic partnerships and synergies with the likes of Azerbajan Airlines, Vodafone, and the cities of Seville (Spain), Llíria (Spain), Dubai (UAE), and Linz (Austria). The company is also working on AAV solutions tailored to emergency medical services and firefighting.

Then we also have the Samson Switchblade,[29] which is a *true* flying car, being airworthy and yet able to function as a road car as well. This three-wheeled vehicle is designed to drive and be refueled like a regular car but will need to unfold its wings and tail to take off from a local

---

[25] "EHang 216 Obtained Operational Flight Permit from Civil Aviation Authority of Norway." *News, Ehang*, www.ehang.com/news/613.html (accessed March 5, 2020).

[26] "EHang 216 Obtained Special Flight Operations Certificate from Transport Canada Civil Aviation." *News, Ehang*, www.ehang.com/news/665.html (accessed July 29, 2020).

[27] "EHang Joins European Union's AMU-LED Project to Demonstrate Urban Air Mobility." *News, Ehang*, www.ehang.com/article/p/2.html (accessed January 21, 2021).

[28] "EHang Announces Pricing of Initial Public Offering." *News, Ehang*, www.ehang.com/news/600.html (accessed December 12, 2019).

[29] www.samsonsky.com/specs/

Figure 9.5 Illustration of SkyDrive SD-XX

Credit: Courtesy of SkyDrive

airport. In flying mode, this flying car is anticipated to reach speeds of up to 200 miles per hour at a height of 13,000 feet.

Challenges

Flying cars hold a lot of commercial potential for the future and this prospect is driving the growth of the sector. Yet, one challenge with the concept of *true* flying cars is how to design vehicles that are compact enough to take off from and land on regular road infrastructure—rather than airports or vertiports—and that can perform well as aircraft and as practical road cars.

Nevertheless, with our growing adeptness at microjet technology, miniaturization, and battery technology, it is inevitable that we will soon be able to combine aerial and wheeled mobility systems into practical, compact, and safe mobility platforms that can be as nimble in the air as they are on land. When that day comes, and it surely will, this will open a Pandora's Box to a whole new set of challenges.

The most obvious hurdle will be how to manage the burgeoning air traffic that will arise from the mass adoption of flying cars by everyday consumers. The likely surge in air traffic could be many orders of magnitude greater than conventional air traffic from commercial, cargo, and military aircraft, and may be too much for human air traffic controllers to handle. Thankfully, the enabling technologies for sufficient urban air traffic management systems are already in steady development. These include the usual suspects: AI, high-speed super and quantum computing, high-speed wireless connectivity, and the Internet of Things (IoT).

There are also infrastructural challenges. The proliferation of flying cars and personal AAVs may necessitate complete redesigns of urban transport infrastructure. On a large enough scale, personal flying transport could trigger reductions in the size and scale of roadways in and between city centers, easing our reliance on crude-based road surface materials. Decreased proximity and interaction between vehicular and pedestrian traffic could drastically reduce accidents.

Airplanes: The Shape of Things to Come

Though the current paradigm of tube-shaped airplanes with fixed wings and kerosene-fueled engines has persisted for decades, there have been consistent attempts to look at alternatives. The few successful deviations from the norm have emerged chiefly from the military domain. Recent years, however, are seeing increased nonmilitary interest in alternative airframes, powerplants, and fuels, particularly as airlines seek to reduce running costs and carbon footprints.

Airframes

Two concepts that are receiving major attention are the blended wing body (BWB) and flying wing. Several aviation entities are investigating the potential of these designs for commercial aviation. Flying-wing aircraft have no separate fuselage; everything is designed into the wing structure itself. Blended wing body aircraft, however, feature separate fuselage and wing assemblies but these are blended together in such a way that drag-inducing wing-fuselage intersections are eliminated.

If designed appropriately, BWB fuselages can be aerodynamic enough to contribute significant supplemental lift. This is the major rationale for toying with BWB designs. Manufacturers want to create aircraft that can generate enough lift to carry more passengers with less fuel consumption. It is also probable that blended wing body and flying wing commercial aircraft will be able to fit more passengers and cargo within the comparable lengths or wingspans of conventional tubular aircraft. These factors are all beneficial for airlines and airports that want to increase capacity and still reduce costs.

Airbus has been experimenting with blended wing designs since the 1990s. The Maveric (Model Aircraft for Validation and Experimentation of Robust Innovative Controls) is just the latest scale-model prototype from Airbus. The blended-wing airfoil generates more lift and reduces drag to such an extent that a full-scale model is projected to use 20 percent less fuel than comparable single-aisle jets.[30] Similar models— the X-48, X-48B, and X-48C—built by Boeing and various collaborators like Cranfield Aerospace and NASA in the 2000s,[31] also proved the fuel-saving efficiencies of blended wing designs.[32]

In 2000, a collaboration between Delft University of Technology (TU Delft) and KLM Royal Dutch Airlines (and other partners, including Airbus), resulted in the successful maiden flight of the Flying-V (Figure 9.6), a scaled flight model of an energy-efficient, long-distance aircraft supposed to be comparable to the Airbus A350 in wingspan and passenger capacity. The concept for this vee-shaped aircraft incorporates the cabin, fuel tanks, and cargo hold into the wings and, like the aforementioned Maveric, also promises 20 percent fuel savings.[33]

With research and testing continuing on both sides of the Atlantic, only time will tell whether it will be the Americans, Europeans, or others who first get a commercial blended-wing aircraft into the operation first.

---

[30] Adams, E. 2020. "Airbus' Maveric Brings B-2 Bomber Style to Passenger Jets." *WIRED*, www.wired.com/story/airbus-maveric-blended-wing-jet/ (accessed February 16, 2020).

[31] Parsch, A. 2009. "Boeing X-48." *Appendix 4: Undesignated Vehicles, Directory of U.S. Military Rockets and Missiles. Designation-Systems.Net*, www.designation-systems.net/dusrm/app4/x-48.html (accessed November 24, 2009).

[32] "Boeing's X-48C Completes Flight Tests." *Defense News, UPI*, www.upi.com/Defense-News/2013/04/12/Boeings-X-48C-completes-flight-tests/84741365783426/?ur3=1 (accessed April 12, 2013).

[33] "Successful maiden flight for the TU Delft Flying-V." *News, TUDelft*, www.tudelft.nl/en/2020/tu-delft/successful-maiden-flight-for-the-tu-delft-flying-v/ (accessed September 1, 2020).

Figure 9.6 *Illustration of the Flying-V flying above the sea*

Credit: Henri Werij, TU Delft

In the interim, an American company—Otto Aviation—has built a bullet-shaped, propeller-powered monoplane that maximizes laminar flow to reduce drag. The 6-seater Otto Celera 500L is targeted at the business and private aviation markets and promises 59 percent less drag and lower operating costs than competing light jets like the Beechcraft King Air 350 and Cessna Citation CJ3+. The pusher propeller thrusts the Celera to a cruising speed of 724 kilometers per hour. The aircraft has a range of 8,300 kilometers and costs only 328 dollars to operate per hour. The plane first flew in 2018 and is undergoing testing to acquire FAA certification before commercial deliveries sometime between 2023 and

2025.[34] At the time of writing, the Celera 500L is the most fuel-efficient, commercially viable aircraft in the world.[35]

Powerplants

Current projects to reimagine the airplane are not only restricted to airframes but also to the powerplants that move them. Novel ideas for powerplants are being experimented by large manufacturers and aviation start-ups around the world.

One recent and exciting development in aircraft propulsion that could eliminate fossil fuels from aviation is the brainchild of Chinese scientists at Wuhan University's Institute of Technological Sciences. Their plasma jet engine, like a typical jet engine, uses compressors to pressurize incoming air; but then, instead of mixing the air with fuel and igniting it, it uses high-powered microwaves to ionize the air into plasma, which expands and shoots out the rear, creating massive thrust.[36] Scaled tests of the plasma drive in 2020 were able to lift a one-kilogram steel ball above a quartz tube 24 millimeters in diameter.[37]

This novel way of creating explosive jet thrust without aviation fuel could revolutionize the aerospace industry by providing a viable electric-powered equivalent that is truly comparable to the classic jet engine

---

[34] Hemmerdinger, J. 2020. "Otto Aviation Reveals Celera Business Aircraft with Super-Efficient 'Laminar Flow'." *FlightGlobal*, www.flightglobal.com/airframers/otto-aviation-reveals-celera-business-aircraft-with-super-efficient-laminar-flow/139929.article (accessed August 27,2020).

[35] Steffen, A.D. 2020. "Celera 500L: The World's Most Fuel-Efficient, Commercially Viable Aircraft." *Intelligent Living*, www.intelligentliving.co/celera-500l/ (accessed September 7, 2020).

[36] Makichuk, D. 2020. "Chinese Researchers Create Prototype Plasma Jet Engine." *Asia Times*, https://asiatimes.com/2020/05/chinese-researchers-create-prototype-plasma-jet-engine/ (accessed May 11, 2020).

[37] Zhen, L. 2020. "Chinese Scientists Say Their New Plasma Drive Could One Day Make Green Air Travel a Reality." www.scmp.com/news/china/science/article/3083382/chinese-scientists-say-their-new-plasma-drive-could-one-day-make (accessed May 8, 2020).

in terms of power.[38] There are other possible advantages to such engines beyond just being environmentally friendly. The ability of these engines to run on air without combusting the oxygen within it may enable them to operate at higher altitudes where oxygen levels are too low to sustain conventional jet engines. By raising the operational flight ceiling, plasma jet engines could power a new generation of passenger airplanes that can leverage the lower drag associated with the thinner air of the upper atmosphere to reach supersonic speeds with ease. To be overly optimistic, it is quite possible that this may be our ticket to a sustainable return to commercial supersonic travel. To be conservative, the reality is that there are still many other aerodynamic, design and production factors to consider before the building of such high-altitude hypersonic cruisers can become commercially viable.

On the opposite side of the globe, in the United States, another equally radical, almost unbelievable, propulsion system is emerging: one that is bladeless, almost silent, and has no moving parts. In 2018, engineers at the Massachusetts Institute of Technology (MIT) constructed and tested a light aircraft powered by electroaerodynamic (EAD) thrust, which is sometimes called electric wind or ionic wind.[39] Arrays of anodes and cathodes placed variably before and along small airfoils, constituting the ion drives, ionized nitrogen in the air and attracted it through an electric field toward the rear of the aircraft. The resulting flow of air generated thrust. The miniature EAD aircraft was five meters wide and weighed just 2.5 kilograms, but the ion drives worked.[40] Obviously, EAD propulsion technology is in its infancy and it may be a long time before the concept is improved and scaled up for practical aircraft. This technology will more likely make its way onto drones before passenger aircraft.[41]

---

[38] "Plasma Jet Thrusters Make Push for Propulsion." *The Engineer*, www.theengineer.co.uk/plasma-jet-microwave-wuhan/ (accessed May 6, 2020).

[39] Chu, J. 2018. "MIT Engineers Fly First-Ever Plane with No Moving Parts." *MIT News*, https://news.mit.edu/2018/first-ionic-wind-plane-no-moving-parts-1121 (accessed November 21, 2018).

[40] "First Flight of Ion-Drive Aircraft." *Nature*, www.nature.com/articles/d41586-018-07477-9 (accessed November 21, 2018).

[41] Bogaisky, J. 2018. "First Test of Aircraft with An Ion Drive Points to a Radically Different Future For Aviation." *Forbes*, www.forbes.com/sites/jeremybogaisky/2018/11/30/ion-engine-mit-solid-state-aircraft/?sh=146cd8ef468d (accessed November 30, 2018).

Thoughts

The previously mentioned innovations in airframes and powerplants are just the tip of the iceberg of cutting-edge research into alternative aircraft systems. There is still a monumental amount of ingenuity going into incremental improvements in more traditional airframes and powerplants. These entail better design characteristics and an increased use of light composites in commercial jets, as well as research and development into hydrogen and electric engines. In all likelihood, however, the future of aviation will lean on electricity. Whether using plasma jet engines, ion drives, or electric motors, these systems will rely on electricity and this is the limiting factor on the scalability of these solutions. The energy density of current battery technology needs to improve to make high-capacity batteries powerful enough and light enough to integrate into future aircraft. This could be the primary limiting factor on widespread deployment of electric-powered thrust systems on future passenger aircraft.

Spaceflight

Space exploration is no exemption to the staggering pace of innovation that is pervading through the world. The soaring digital communication needs of the Fourth Industrial Revolution are driving continuing demand for space-based telecommunications satellites and technology. There is no shortage of corporate customers willing to pay top dollar to space agencies to deliver their proprietary technologies into orbit. Furthermore, the U.S. National Aeronautics and Space Administration (NASA) and other prominent space agencies from rival countries have renewed their interests in manned expeditions and have launched several programs to get people on a space station, to the Moon, or to Mars. All of these are driving competition in the spaceflight market and providing the economic push for private space contractors to innovate better and cheaper space technologies.

In the United States, NASA has a handful of programs driving its agenda for the next few years, including the Commercial Crew Program and the Artemis program. To execute these programs, NASA has forged strong partnerships with private contractors. The Commercial Crew

Program (CCP), which began in 2011, entails the development of cheaper, more dependable routine transportation for crew to and from the International Space Station (ISS). NASA's two main partners on the program are the century-old aerospace giant, Boeing, and the radical, barely two-decade-old start-up, SpaceX, owned by business magnate, Elon Musk.

The Artemis program is focused on the development of technologies for returning people—most especially, women—to the Moon for unprecedented exploration campaigns by 2024. For this, NASA is collaborating with the likes of Lockheed Martin, Airbus Defence and Space, SpaceX, and Blue Origin, which was founded by Jeff Bezos in 2000.[42]

The range of recent and ongoing innovations by private aerospace contractors such as SpaceX and Blue Origin are staggering. Young aerospace start-ups are approaching spaceflight with new ways of thinking and are harnessing a wealth of emerging technologies such as AI, 3D printing, and IoT to change the way space technology is designed, manufactured, and operated. These often result in cheaper, safer, and more reliable spacecraft, and consistently bring down the cost of spaceflight. The growing integration of reusability into space technology is also improving the economic viability of the industry.

But space exploration is no longer just about the United States, Europe, or Russia. In other parts of the globe, a host of countries are also sending up unmanned missions to space, the Moon, and Mars. These include China and the United Arab Emirates. Indeed, a 21st-century space race is picking up speed. In the long term, a space race is good for society because, invariably, technological breakthroughs in space exploration permeate into terrestrial products, making our lives better and creating new lines of business.

SpaceX

No discussion on the modern space industry would be complete without a special mention of the marvelous achievements of the pioneering

---

[42] Drake, N. 2021. "The Future of Spaceflight—From Orbital Vacations to Humans on Mars." *National Geographic*, www.nationalgeographic.com/science/article/future-spaceflight (accessed April 26, 2021).

start-up, Space Exploration Technologies Corp. (SpaceX).[43] Elon Musk founded SpaceX in 2002 and eventually headquartered it in Hawthorne, California, after a brief stint in nearby El Segundo. Musk's ultimate aim is to make spaceflight safer and cheaper, and to facilitate the colonization of Mars, making mankind a multiplanetary civilization.[44]

SpaceX quickly delved into developing the Falcon range of orbital launch vehicles and after three initial failures, achieved the successful launch into Earth orbit of the small-lift Falcon 1 launch vehicle in September 2008. This made Falcon 1 the world's first privately built liquid fuel rocket to achieve Earth orbit.[45] Soon, the company jumped into the development of the heavier Falcon 9—a reusable, VTOL lift vehicle—which it successfully launched in June 2010, carrying a mockup of the upcoming Dragon spacecraft.

SpaceX's forthcoming Dragon spacecraft were to be a range of reusable crewed or cargo spacecraft. In December 2010, Dragon 1 made its maiden flight into orbit and was successfully recovered back to earth.[46] In May 2012, a cargo Dragon achieved a rendezvous with the International Space Station. Since then, Dragons have been regularly resupplying cargo to the ISS for NASA. Then in 2020, a new crewed version, Dragon 2 (Figure 9.7), successfully launched two NASA astronauts to the ISS. SpaceX was now the world's first private space company to launch a crewed spacecraft into space.[47]

---

[43] www.spacex.com/

[44] Musk, E. 2017. "Making Humans a Multi-Planetary Species." *New Space* 5, no. 2, 46–61. http://doi.org/10.1089/space.2017.29009.emu

[45] "SpaceX Successfully Launches Falcon 1 to Orbit." *Commercial Crew & Cargo*, NASA, www.nasa.gov/offices/c3po/home/spacex_falcon1_flight_4.html (accessed September 28, 2008).

[46] NASA. "SpaceX Launches Success with Falcon 9/Dragon Flight." *Commercial Crew & Cargo*, www.nasa.gov/offices/c3po/home/spacexfeature.html (accessed December 9, 2010).

[47] Howell, E. 2020. "SpaceX's Dragon: First Private Spacecraft to Reach the Space Station." *Space.com*, www.space.com/18852-spacex-dragon.html (accessed August 10, 2020).

Figure 9.7 The unveiling of Crew Dragon 2 (taken May 29, 2014)

Credit: SpaceX

The company is currently building and testing its huge Starship[48] space vehicles (Figure 9.8), which will be launched by a reusable first stage called the Super Heavy. The massive Starship, which is designed to carry over a hundred tons into space, is the most powerful launch vehicle in history. The Starship system is intended to enable missions to Earth orbit, the Moon, Mars, and beyond.

Figure 9.8 Starship SN10 in high-altitude flight test (March 4, 2021)

Credit: SpaceX

---

[48] www.spacex.com/vehicles/starship/

Another pioneering project of SpaceX is Starlink,[49] a large constellation of small Internet satellites in low Earth orbit that make fast, affordable broadband available to the entire globe. Space X currently has over 1,320 Starlink satellites in orbit.[50] Starlink is now operational and available to a limited but growing number of users, as the company moves toward its intended constellation size of up to 42,000 satellites.[51]

SpaceX is acclaimed for its private spaceflight milestones and its groundbreaking development of the Merlin, Kestrel, Raptor, Draco, and SuperDraco rocket engines. The achievements of this roughly two-decade-old company are a testament to the power of vertical integration, emerging production technologies, and novel business concepts to drive affordable technology and commercial viability in any industry, even one as expensive as spaceflight.

---

[49] www.starlink.com/

[50] Clark, S. 2021. "SpaceX Launches 25th Mission for Starlink Internet Network." *Spaceflight Now*, https://spaceflightnow.com/2021/03/24/spacex-launches-25th-mission-to-build-out-starlink-internet-network/ (accessed March 24, 2021).

[51] Huang, M.Y., B. Hunt, and D. Mosher. 2021. "What Elon Musk's 42,000 Starlink Satellites Could do for—and to—Planet Earth." *Business Insider*, www.businessinsider.com/how-elon-musk-42000-starlink-satellites-earth-effects-stars-2020-10?IR=T (accessed March 4, 2021).

CHAPTER 10

The Flexible Workplace

The nature of work and workplaces has evolved dramatically over the course of the three Industrial Revolutions, resulting in the status quo that pertains today. Agrarian societies gave way to the highly organized manufacturing industries typical of the First Industrial Revolution, which then acquiesced to the increased automation and digitization of the Second and Third Industrial Revolutions. Depending on factors such as geography and demography, modern workplaces vary greatly, exhibiting a mix of working conditions characteristic of the First, Second, or Third Industrial Revolutions, as well as radical new-age work practices. This chapter focuses primarily on cutting-edge human resource dynamics and on organizations that are adopting revolutionary ways of fostering and measuring productivity.

Telepresence

Progressive corporate cultures tend to embrace technologies that create flexible conditions for meetings and collaboration. These include platforms for video and web conferencing such as Zoom, FaceTime (Apple), Teams (Microsoft), TeamViewer, Adobe Connect, Skype, Google Hangouts, and Cisco Webex. These and other related platforms enable employees to work remotely with increased efficiency.

Travel restrictions and social distance protocols linked to the Covid-19 pandemic of 2020 and 2021 have gone a long way to drive the patronage of these products. Remote work can be extremely beneficial in creating convenience (work–life balance) and keeping employees isolated and safe during pandemics or local epidemics. While the move to flexible remote working models has been in play for quite some time within forward-thinking companies, the Covid-19 pandemic forced the mass adoption of work from home (WFH) by many businesses. With so many enterprises having tasted the benefits of WFH arrangements, it is possible that many will not desire a full return to full office life. WFH reduces the need for expensive daily commutes whose costs add up in money and in time. Flexible working hours make it possible for some companies to spend less on large offices with dedicated seating, and to rather have flexible *hot* desks, which can be commandeered by employees when necessary.

In March 2021, the Ford Motor Company announced that 30,000 of its staff across the globe would be able to extend working from home arrangements for the foreseeable future, coming into the office only for special meetings and in-person projects.[1] With the unavoidable migration to hybrid or flexible remote working arrangements, the challenge then becomes how to effectively stimulate and monitor remote productivity. How do we also ensure that remoteness does not eventuate in disengagement? In times of pandemics and health-related restrictions, how do we foster collaboration while reducing interaction? Some developers are looking at enterprise productivity apps to solve this conundrum.

There are already many software solutions in the market for employees to remotely collaborate on shared digital assets such as documents, graphics, and other deliverables. But with the new norm brought on by the Covid-19 pandemic, the market for related solutions is bound to grow. Seamless teamwork on project files and deliverables while in separate remote locations is of value to employees and companies looking to speed up and simplify the collaborative process.

Telecontrol

While white-collar roles and nontechnical fields can benefit greatly from remote work using only video conferencing to collaborate, mechanical or engineering fields that require physical collaboration cannot benefit from work-from-home arrangements as easily. This is where telecontrol comes in, by enabling productive industries to also be run remotely. Conventional video conferencing platforms focus on sight and sound, but

---

[1] Krisher, T and C. Rugaber. 2021. "Will Work from Home Outlast Virus? Ford's Move Suggests Yes," *Yahoo! News*, https://news.yahoo.com/home-outlast-virus-fords-move-133040039.html (accessed March 17, 2021).

computer scientists are moving beyond those two senses and creating technologies that can simulate other senses like touch (via haptic feedback) and that can simulate physical movements remotely.

Telecontrol—the remote control of systems, robotic arms, and equipment—is currently helping in the field of telemedicine, where surgeries can be performed by remotely operated robots, controlled by absent experts. This makes surgeries possible even when experts are unable to commute on time or commute at all. The military also uses telecontrol in the remote piloting of some unmanned aerial vehicles, thereby eliminating threat of harm or loss of life from combat situations.

Distance Learning and Development

With the fast pace of global technological progress, many edgy companies now prescribe regular, mandatory training to keep personnel up to date with trends within their industries. Invariably, many of these primers come in online formats for distance learning. Several leading knowledge and skills providers such as LinkedIn, edX, and Coursera offer flexible online solutions, but these tend to be tailored toward individual learning experiences. With the Covid-19 pandemic and some schools being forced to close down, platforms like Google Classroom that enable effective group learning and feature participant-to-participant communication are coming to prominence. There is a growing market for analogous solutions, moving forward.

Such platforms are beneficial for companies because they can foster group engagement with employees working remotely from home and thereby boost morale, and consequently, motivation, productivity, job satisfaction, and retention. They also serve as effective channels for public employee recognition, which is also essential to maintaining motivation and engagement.

As technologies for improving the art of work continue to be deployed, so also the field of human resource management will by necessity encounter increased technical sophistication. Enterprise HR solutions will get better at monitoring employee productivity and metrics such as engagement and satisfaction.

CHAPTER 11

Managing Innovation and Technology Development

R&D for the New Age

Though the deployment and commercialization of new technologies are often highly publicized and forced down our throats via media channels, the inner workings of the engineering ecosystems that develop these innovations largely remain masked from the public eye. Like the ancient, smithing dwarves of Germanic folklore, the talented craftsmen of modern times dwell in an obscure world while their creations become all the rave in society, moving mankind forward one small step at a time.

But how does modern innovation actually happen? Where do the unseen armies of invention lurk and work? Where are these geeky research worlds? Who are the people who work there? Who manages them? What educational and career paths must one take to enter these mysterious realms of creation? How does one become a tech developer, R&D manager, or innovation manager?

Throughout the ages, innovation has emanated largely from talented individuals, some with help from rich benefactors. But, with the increasing impact and profitability of new technologies during the First Industrial Revolution, it was inevitable that the process of research and development would become formalized into organized entities within academia or into corporate structures such as fully fledged companies or research divisions within companies.

This formalization, which helped standardize intellectual property rights and furnish engineers with large budgets, played a big role in the Second and Third Industrial Revolutions, and helped create our current paradigm where countless companies have dedicated innovation teams or departments.

The persistence of many civil, regional, and world wars brought to the fore, the grave security implications of unbridled or weaponized innovation. Key companies were increasingly engaged by military and defense agencies and were able to create special departments within their corporate structures, which would work on classified defense contracts. Typical examples are Boeing Phantom Works[1] and Lockheed Martin's Advanced Development Programs—better known as Skunk Works[2]—which have long track records of defense contracts with the U.S. government.

Innovation Labs, Hubs, Accelerators, and Technology Centers

Over the past few decades, as companies, individuals, politicians, and venture capitalists have grown aware of the benefits of the innovation process—and not just the products that arise from it—innovation labs have become accepted as essential conduits for new ideas that can maintain an entity's competitive advantage.

Many companies are opening innovation labs, which are dedicated entities or business units purposed for the development of cutting-edge ideas and working prototypes of products and services. Innovation labs are sometimes known as hubs, accelerators, or incubators. These labs are set up with a variety of objectives: to stay ahead of disruptive trends in the market and thereby protect a parent company from competition; to create radical new products and services for the parent company; to attract and groom amazing talent; to identify, collaborate with, and/or absorb competitive start-ups; or to serve as a testimonial for a company's foresight and modernity.

Innovation labs can be structured in a variety of ways. They can be created internally, drawing on staff from within an organization, or they can be separate offshoots that operate independently with their own

---

[1] www.boeing.com/defense/phantom-works/

[2] www.lockheedmartin.com/en-us/who-we-are/business-areas/aeronautics/skunkworks.html

dedicated workforce. Innovation labs can also be standalone entities not tied to any parent company and which can then collaborate freely with companies, academia, investors, individuals, and governments at will, on a wide range of objectives.

Typically, accelerators will generate a concept, pilot it, and iterate until the prototype is integrated into mainstream business or launched into the market. This birthing of ideas and incubation of concepts often involves ideation, market research, and cross-functional collaboration to create a working proof-of-concept.

There are many notable examples of impactful innovation labs and hubs in multiple sectors across the globe. Boston-based Solaris Labs is an innovation hub belonging to Liberty Mutual and runs out of a WeWork, which is any shared, flexible, innovation workspace created by the commercial real estate company, WeWork. Solaris Labs is making waves by collaborating with universities and engaging or incubating start-ups in and around Boston.

SC Ventures is an innovation offshoot of Standard Chartered Bank in Hong Kong and is housed in the eXellerator Lab, which sits on Standard Chartered Tower's ninth floor, a space purposely redesigned and renovated by WeWork.[3] Ideas developed at the eXellerator Lab have led to projects such as the development of a web chatbot and the reworking of the bank's call centers and mobile app.

Booz Allen Hamilton Inc. has entered the fray by setting up an ecosystem of innovation hub communities called iHubs across the United States. Booz Allen's iHub Network includes innovation centers in Washington, D.C.; at Annapolis Junction in Central Maryland; at Downtown Crossing in Boston; in Austin, Texas; in San Francisco; and in Downtown Seattle. Through these iHubs, Booz Allen has formed working synergies with academia, start-ups, Fortune 500 companies, and investors. Some noteworthy allies include Techstars, Amazon, Microsoft, and Tableau.[4]

---

[3] Green, N. 2021. "What is an Innovation Lab?" *WeWork*, www.wework. com/ideas/professional-development/management-leadership/innovation-labs (accessed February 24, 2021).

[4] "Innovation Hubs." *Booz Allen*, www.boozallen.com/about/innovation/innovation-hubs.html (accessed April 26, 2021).

Some innovation hubs are set up or fostered by governments and/ or investors to boost general economic development within their cities. Barcelona Tech City is housed in a converted shipping warehouse called Pier 01 on the Mediterranean coast. This private, nonprofit association boasts 500 members, one of which is the City of Barcelona, and attracts local and foreign investment to the Barcelona area. Barcelona Tech City offers reasonable rent rates to start-ups; the innovation units of giants like Volkswagen, La Caixa Bank; and venture capital firms like ANTAI.[5]

Some innovation hubs tied to tech prefer to be housed in technology cities so that they can be near the tech giants they hope will collaborate with or acquire them. Technology centers and cities have burgeoned in number and include famous and up-and-coming examples, including Silicon Valley (California), Dulles Technology Corridor (Virginia), Hsinchu Science Park (Taiwan), Silicon Alley (New York), Silicon Corridor (UK), Bangalore (India), HITEC City (Hyderabad, India), Dubai Internet City, Dubai Silicon Oasis, Singapore Science Park, Yabacon Valley (Lagos, Nigeria), Kansai Science City (Japan), and Digital Media City (Seoul, South Korea).

Individual Innovators

Many companies, business units, and corporate entities have been celebrated throughout this book for their radical impacts on our world. AT&T, Bell Labs, IBM, GE, Tesla, 3M, Microsoft, and Intel are just a few of the thousands of industrial innovators that are moving us forward. It is interesting to note, however, that with the increasing democratization of ICT and finance, and with the amazing capabilities of tools and equipment in the consumer market, innovation is still firmly within the reach of hobbyists and enthusiasts. Now, more than ever, *anyone* can invent creations, garner attention, and then crowdsource funds to scale up without corporate backing.

---

[5] Greenwald, M. 2018. "A New Wave of Innovation Hubs Sweeping the World." www.forbes.com/sites/michellegreenwald/2018/04/02/a-new-wave-of-innovation-hubs-sweeping-the-world/?sh=4ec952881265 (accessed April 2, 2018).

Typical examples of potent individual innovators are the communities of private enthusiasts who are pushing the boundaries of 3D printing by building their own printers, using an ever-growing assortment of materials, and by challenging each other to print the unthinkable. Other private inventors emerge from communities of custom-car buffs, private aviation hobbyists, and cryptographic geniuses like the mysterious Satoshi Nakakoto, the creator of blockchain and Bitcoin.

Nonetheless, with companies and venture capitalists on the constant lookout for new ideas and stark, raving talent, successful private inventors and innovators do not operate alone for long. They regularly gain traction only to be quickly and forcibly collaborated with or bought out. Some privately conceived innovations are so risky and untested that they are way beyond *cutting-edge*: they are *bleeding-edge*. Occasionally, some of these conceptions come to light when their creators form ad hoc teams to compete in innovation challenges or competitions such as the various XPRIZE challenges,[6] the Hult Prize,[7] 3M's Invent a New Future (INF) challenge, Microsoft's Imagine Cup,[8] AIF's Innovation Prize for Africa,[9] Regeneron Science Talent Search,[10] and IXL Innovation Olympics.[11]

The Modern CTO

How is innovation managed? In hardware-related industries, R&D departments are mostly headed by R&D managers or Chief R&D Officers. In business-oriented innovation departments, this role usually goes to an innovation manager and ultimately, the more senior chief technical officer (CTO).

With the ever-changing business landscape, innovation managers must have certain critical skillsets to be exemplary and deliver results. The tendency of emerging technologies to cut across multiple fields implies

---

[6] www.xprize.org/

[7] www.hultprize.org/

[8] https://imaginecup.microsoft.com/en-US

[9] http://africaninnovation.org/

[10] www.regeneron.com/responsibility/sts-isef

[11] www.ixlcenter.io/

that ardent innovation managers must be wide-read deep thinkers with working knowledge of many disciplines and experience with multisectoral projects. They can come from a variety or combination of backgrounds but ideally need some business and/or science and engineering background from any discipline.

Project management competencies can serve one well in this capacity as one balances the slow pace of engineering with hard deadlines. Innovation managers must be able to tread the fine line of balancing the unbridled freedom of innovating outside the box with the specific, tangible—and often, commercial—objectives of the parent organization. Simply put, innovation managers must be able to make haste, slowly.

Additionally, it helps if innovation managers are change management champions as this helps them to anticipate how the deployment of their products will impact an organization. Such knowledge of institutional inertia and organizational processes will help them incorporate remedial measures when developing products. But these are just generalizations. There are still professionals who come from completely unrelated backgrounds but who make amazing innovation managers because of their critical thinking skills and communication or people management skills.

One very important trait of fantastic innovation managers is that they must be open to receiving bottom-up feedback from their reports who are working directly with the innovation. Open lines of communication ensure that problems are quickly identified and communicated to the relevant personnel to mitigate or deal with them.

CHAPTER 12

What Now? Thriving in the Fourth Industrial Revolution

Congratulations on getting through this book and on managing to imbibe basic knowledge about the workings of many of mankind's latest technologies. Looking back at the amazing range of emerging innovations making their way into so many industries, you may indeed agree with those experts who posit that we are on the brink of—or already in—a fourth industrial revolution. This next wave of change will almost certainly herald new energy technologies, societal and workforce shifts, and a further melding of the digital and physical worlds.

The transformations fostered by this revolution will benefit some, while negatively affecting others, in countless ways. The rise of artificial intelligence (AI) and its mass adoption across numerous spheres may exacerbate the rate of obsolescence of many job types and skill sets. While the rise of robotics and automation may have chiefly impacted blue-collar factory-based jobs, the rise of AI has the potential to invalidate a range of white-collar roles. The upsurge of leaner, additive manufacturing through nanotechnology and 3D printing will likely diminish bulky, outdated subtractive industries and their concomitant workforces.

Governments and centralized regulatory authorities around the world will feel the brunt of blockchain and the democratization of data authentication. Decentralized consensus will become the order of the day, fostering transparency and infallibility in many facets of the public sector. Attractive career prospects for financial professionals may begin to swing from positions in large gatekeeper institutions to roles in niche firms speculating in mixed portfolios of crypto assets with conventional holdings. Meanwhile, tech jobs will continue to gain prominence.

And as the digital world continues to swell, so will the arts and entertainment industries. As digital entertainment channels grow in reach, the earning potential from involvement in this sector will skyrocket, providing supplementary income streams to many. Indie artists, niche talents, freelance journalists, and the like will see rising returns.

The energy revolutions of Industry 4.0 will make it the age of the inexhaustibles. Cheap, unlimited power will fuel a new paradigm of unbridled mobility and mobile pastimes. The recovering climate and improved environmental stewardship will have unfathomable ripple effects on our health and the survival of other species.

The omnipresence and pervasiveness of IoT and other technologies will improve our quality of life and engender unprecedented utility and convenience, taking laboriousness out of our domestic and public lifestyles. Also, there will be unrivaled symbiosis between our enhanced digital world and the physical realm as our augmented reality lifestyles will allow us to remain in both worlds at the same time. There may be massive reductions in public expenditure on physical infrastructure like road signage and traffic lights as navigation and informational signage migrate to digital.

And while the Digital or Third Industrial Revolution may seem to some to have created a world where people take company for granted, Industry 4.0's promulgation of virtual worlds and pandemic-related social distancing protocols will create a society where physical interaction is seen as a privilege; a world where we value opportunities to share physical proximity and spend time together.

The field of business will continue to evolve as products and services break barriers and reach into new frontiers unparalleled in the history of man. The commercialization of space travel and the provision of off-planet services like Internet connectivity will create new cosmic markets. There will be new waves of outsourcing models for decentralizing production and supply chains. Public–private partnerships (PPPs) will continue enabling the penetration of private business into erstwhile prohibited industries such as defense, space travel, and government. As the privatization of spaceflight grows more successful, it will usher in a new age of powerful private space firms, following in the stead of Elon Musk and SpaceX.

The field of human resources will also change. There will be a continuing focus on talent and versatility. The growing variance between low-skill low-pay jobs and high-skill high-pay jobs may create social tensions. Also, as life expectancy rises and institutional knowledge becomes more valuable, retirement ages will rise. And for the retired, a growing plethora of platforms for private consulting and freelance engagement will bring an end to the retirement of the mind.

Progressive Attitudes to Innovation

All of the previous predictions may be mere possibilities, but what *is* certain is that Industry 4.0 will cause radical shifts in human resources across most industries. As with the three previous industrial revolutions, these changes in workforces are inevitable. To be ready for these changes, astute professionals must commit to a growth mindset and adopt progressive attitudes toward tech and innovation. With the growing likelihood of an impending era of HR that is preoccupied with intellectual talent and soft skills, there is no such thing as being too old to learn this or that, unless one is planning to start physical feats such as training for Olympic gymnastics; in which case, then yes, one may be physically too old to start at 50. But even then ... who knows?

There are an assortment of online courses, certifications, and unconventional learning platforms one can utilize to get with the program, so to speak. Many are easier on the pocket than in-person learning but can be intense and require self-discipline. They can be game changers on a resume for people looking to stay relevant to the times and can have an immediate impact on one's career prospects. There are also a range of trendy industry conferences, expositions, and exhibitions for unconventional and emerging tech that one can start attending, to stay abreast with current trends.

As the rate of innovation continues to outpace industry adoption and regulation, staying relevant in the job market of Industry 4.0 will require a lifestyle of continual learning and development (L&D). It is my wish that this book inspires you to contemplate an L&D plan that meets your own unique ambitions.

About the Author

George Baffour is a mixed-race German Ghanaian and a grandson of the late, great Dr. Robert Patrick Baffour, OBE, OV, a celebrated Ghanaian academic and inventor. He holds an MBA (with distinction) from Hult International Business School and preceding BSc and MPhil degrees in oceanography and fisheries science, respectively, from the University of Ghana.

George is deeply passionate about science, technology, and innovation. He began his working career as an assistant research scientist at Water Research Institute (WRI)—one of 13 institutes under the Republic of Ghana's Council for Scientific and Industrial Research (CSIR)—before taking on engagements in business and media. While pursuing his MBA at Hult IBS, he was a winner *(Team DUBAInnovators)* of the *2015 Emirates NBD Future Intelligence Challenge* in Dubai and a global winner *(Team 7Sigma)* of *3M Invent a New Future Challenge 2016* at 3M Headquarters in Minnesota, USA.

He is the author of the 2008 science-fiction/fantasy novel, *Bubble Joe and his fantastic journeys to Zapokrepit in the Land of the Day and a Half*, and the 2018 science-fiction/romance novelette, *From Japan With Love Beyond Time*, which features concepts such as artificial intelligence, augmented reality, autonomous mobility, and the shared economy. In West Africa, George is also known as an actor, songwriter, and producer—under the stage name, *SoulKnight-Jazz*—with screen credits in several Ghanaian and Nigerian film/TV productions.

Index

www.ingramcontent.com/pod-product-compliance
Lightning Source LLC
Chambersburg PA
CBHW061306220326
41599CB00026B/4757